CAPE EDITIONS 15

General Editor: NATHANIEL TARN

Journeys
Günter Eich

Two Radio Plays:
The Rolling Sea at Setúbal
The Year Lacertis
translated from the German
by Michael Hamburger

JONATHAN CAPE
THIRTY BEDFORD SQUARE
LONDON

First published in Great Britain 1968
by Jonathan Cape Ltd, 30 Bedford Square, London, WC1
Translated from the German *Die Brandung vor Setúbal*
and *Das Jahr Lazertis*
© 1958 by Suhrkamp Verlag, Frankfurt am Main
Translation © 1968 by Jonathan Cape Ltd

SBN Paperback edition 224 61338 3
    Hardback edition 224 61337 5

Printed and bound in Great Britain
by Richard Clay (The Chaucer Press), Ltd
Bungay, Suffolk

The Rolling
Sea at
Setúbal

VOICES

PEDRO, Catarina's servant

FELIPE, landlord of the inn

OJAO, servant of Camoens

LORD CHAMBERLAIN

CATARINA DE ATAIDE

ROSITA, her maid

LANDLORD'S WIFE

THE MOTHER OF CAMOENS

Rosita enters Dona Catarina's bedroom.

ROSITA. Your chocolate, Dona Catarina.

CATARINA. My chocolate. (*She stretches and sits up.*)

ROSITA. The tray on the coverlet, so that it touches her dressing-gown.

CATARINA. Carry out my orders, Rosita: don't repeat them like a parrot. Ten o'clock?

ROSITA. Exactly.

CATARINA. It can't be exactly so.

ROSITA. It struck the moment I came through the door.

CATARINA. Came through the door? When you were outside or in? On the first stroke or the tenth? How carelessly you express yourself. Didn't I tell you to call me so that I should hear the tenth stroke? I didn't hear it.

ROSITA. It's difficult, Dona Catarina. It's never really worked since my first year. Then I'd wait at the door for the fifth stroke before pressing down the handle. But I don't know how it came about, whether it was the clockwork that changed, or my patience. The fact is I couldn't bring it off any longer. And if I opened the door on the fourth stroke, there was the danger that a skin might form on the chocolate.

CATARINA. Disgusting!

ROSITA. To tell you the truth, it's been getting worse

7

and worse every year. In fact more than once I've had palpitations when I reached the door.

CATARINA. I expect there are other reasons for that, Rosita. You were seventeen when you came to me, and you've been with me for five years. It's the age for strong palpitations.

ROSITA. Not only palpitations, though. My teeth chatter too, and I'm afraid I shall drop the tray.

CATARINA. Your symptoms bore me. And I never heard anything like it from your predecessor, who was in my service for twelve years.

ROSITA. That's no wonder, Dona Catarina, since she had no teeth left.

CATARINA. Enough small talk. Remove the cup. The weather?

ROSITA. Dull.

CATARINA. The sea?

ROSITA. Rolling as ever.

CATARINA. Quiet! (*A pause*) Yes, it's rolling as ever. That's a comfort. Do you know how I feel when I hear that sound?

ROSITA. You've told me, Dona Catarina : nearer to God.

CATARINA. How unspeakably silly that sounds when you say it.

ROSITA. It sounds silly as – (*She stops short, startled.*)

CATARINA. As what?

ROSITA. No, nothing.

CATARINA. Sometimes there's something insolent about you – a rebellious strain.

ROSITA (*candidly*). Oh, no; certainly not.

CATARINA. What's that stain on the coverlet? Everything is getting spoiled and filthy, because you girls pay no attention.

ROSITA. It's red wine, Dona Catarina; yesterday's.

CATARINA (*taken aback*). Red wine? My own doing? (*Since Rosita keeps silent*) How much did I drink?

ROSITA. You left the dregs of two litres.

CATARINA (*sadly*). Well, I left the dregs anyway. (*After a pause*) The strange thing is that I couldn't bear to hear it at first. I used to put my hands over my ears.

ROSITA. The rolling sea, you mean?

CATARINA. It seemed like the very epitome of my exile. Oh, my ears were full of gay laughter from the royal palace, tender words from the trellised walks in the park, verses –

ROSITA. Today's poem is: 'On the Banks of the Mondego he thinks of his Natercia.'

CATARINA. But twenty-seven years are enough to transmute the crackle of Hell's flames into the soothing murmur of divine forgiveness.

ROSITA (*uncertain*). You're quoting?

CATARINA. To transmute hatred into love.

ROSITA. And the love into what, if I may make so free as to ask?

CATARINA. You may not make so free. (*She sobs.*)

ROSITA (*helpless*). Dona Catarina!

CATARINA (*calmly*). What poem?

ROSITA. The third in Volume II.

CATARINA. Don't pretend you can read. Pedro is having no end of trouble with you.

ROSITA. And so are you, Dona Catarina.

CATARINA. I must admit, my child, that it isn't one of the regular duties of a lady's maid to recite verses. Stand over there, next to the wardrobe.

ROSITA. And gaze out of the window on to the sea.

CATARINA. Don't say it, Rosita, do it!

ROSITA. Few days divide us: seven to speak plain.
        Like seven waves they travel with the tide,
        Mere flecks upon those waters deep and wide,
        As endlessly I tell myself – in vain!

        For I can set no limits to the pain
        Of this brief span of absence; nor abide
        The single glance, the single kiss denied,
        And of their lack most grievously complain.

        No measure now is valid, but thine own,
        Natercia, for eternity and time,
        The glance, the kiss, the grief that fills my
           rhyme.

        Both clock and calendar I have outgrown,
        The very sun and moon thine eyes eclipse:
        Eternity begins upon thy lips.

CATARINA. Eternity – all right. But twenty-seven years?

ROSITA. It's difficult to recite something one doesn't understand.

CATARINA. It's because you don't understand it that you have the ability. You recite the poem excellently, my child.

ROSITA. In that case it must be the wardrobe, and the oblique view of the sea.

CATARINA. Why don't you understand it, by the way? How could anyone fail to understand it?

ROSITA. I don't understand the feelings he's put into rhymes.

CATARINA (*disconcerted*). Oh? (*After a pause*) There really is something rebellious about you. Ideas of that kind are not fitting for servants.

ROSITA. I beg your pardon, Dona Catarina.

CATARINA. Oh, fiddlesticks! Let's begin a revolutionary conversation. So the rhymes –

ROSITA. And Natercia. Why does he say Natercia, when your name is Catarina?

CATARINA. In the course of the years I've begun to wonder whether my name isn't Natercia.

ROSITA. But at that time –

CATARINA. Yes, true enough, at that time my name was still Catarina. We must proceed methodically, my child. The rhymes and Natercia are two entirely different matters. We mustn't confuse them. The point of the rhymes is that they're contrary to nature.

ROSITA (*uncomprehending*). Ah!

CATARINA. Because human virtue begins where God's creature rises above mere crude nature. What do feelings amount to, after all? Skin rubbing against skin; the milkmaids and the mill-hands do that too. It's only when feelings begin to rhyme, Rosita; that's something.

ROSITA. Ah!

CATARINA. Do you follow me? (*Rosita is silent.*) I can read the questions in your obdurate eyes. How unseemly a pretty face becomes when it stares at an older one, how coarse! Imagine me holding my nose and lifting the hem of my dress as I go down the steps in the yard, where the pigs squelch and slobber over their troughs, and the mules drop their apples.

ROSITA. Yes, Dona Catarina, for our sort there is only nature.

CATARINA. And for me too, Rosita, for me too. Don't be offended.

ROSITA. To go back to the pigs: we leave them in the dirt and blame them for stinking.

CATARINA (*taking no notice*). No, I can find no rhymes, no more than you can. I am nothing, I am something only through him, near him, beside him, with him – far from him –

ROSITA (*condoling*). Dear Dona Catarina …

CATARINA. Never mind. It all comes from having allowed you to talk about rhymes. It didn't occur to me how dangerous a topic it is.

ROSITA. And Natercia?

CATARINA. I fear that's another. Well, let's try all the same. Remove the tray and begin to do my hair. What do you think of my hair?

ROSITA. It's very lovely still.

CATARINA (*doubtful*). Do you think so? I fancy it looks as though the moths have got into it.

ROSITA. I think that hair and hair-styles are something I know quite a lot about.

CATARINA. That's your kind of rhyme.

ROSITA (*laughing happily*). Yes, Dona Catarina.

CATARINA. On the other hand, he called me Natercia because no one was to know whom he meant by the name.

ROSITA. I see. No one knew, then?

CATARINA. At first no one knew.

ROSITA. And if he'd kept the poems to himself?

CATARINA. Rosita! Would he have become Portugal's greatest poet in that case? Should we be sitting here, talking about him?

ROSITA. No, but you might have had children and grandchildren now. (*Hurriedly, as though trying to blot out this sentence*) I can just imagine it. It

would be just like when the hen has laid an egg.
Shall I sweep up your hair higher still?

(CATARINA *utters a scream*.)

Did I hurt you, Dona Catarina?

CATARINA. I can see the cup in the looking-glass.

ROSITA (*hurriedly*). Perhaps we should try a new hair-style –

CATARINA. It's the cup with the lily pattern.

ROSITA. If we swept up your hair on the sides –

CATARINA (*sharply*). I am speaking of the cup.

ROSITA (*uncertain*). Yes, of course.

CATARINA. Well?

ROSITA. Yes, it's the cup with the lily pattern.

CATARINA. But I had ordered the rose pattern. Didn't Pedro tell you?

ROSITA. It's possible, madam.

CATARINA. Possible?

ROSITA. Or rather impossible. The cup with the rose pattern was broken – by my predecessor.

CATARINA. Your predecessor? You've been with me for five years. What you're telling me is that for just that time I've been living under the delusion that I drink my morning chocolate out of the rose cup.

ROSITA. Is that such a serious matter?

CATARINA. Not serious, but full of implications.

ROSITA. If I may make so free as to ask another question : Did he always call you Natercia?

CATARINA. That's strange, isn't it?

ROSITA. Who would think of such a thing! Only a poet.

CATARINA. I'm speaking of the cup, and the five years. The thought is like a mist, but one knows that everything will be clearer when it's lifted. What did you say about him?

ROSITA. Did he always call you Natercia?

CATARINA. In the poems, that goes without saying.

ROSITA. And elsewhere too, at times?

CATARINA. And elsewhere too at times.

ROSITA. I like the idea that he called you Natercia even when you were alone together. Though there was nothing to conceal then, and though it didn't rhyme with anything.

CATARINA (*irritated*). Yes, that's true. Why did he do it, in that case?

ROSITA. Perhaps because it was contrary to nature.

CATARINA. I'm beginning to confuse the name with the pattern on the cup.

ROSITA. Perhaps he did it for no reason at all.

CATARINA. For no reason?

ROSITA. Just like that – as a kind of game.

CATARINA (*bewildered*). A kind of game?

ROSITA. Your hair is done. How do you like it?

CATARINA. Call Pedro.

ROSITA (*opens the door*). Pedro!

CATARINA. Did we never mention the pattern on the cup in all these years?

ROSITA. Oh yes, Dona Catarina, but you never actually asked about it.

CATARINA. In that case I allowed myself to be deceived.

ROSITA. I didn't know it was so important to you.

CATARINA. Nor did I know it. (*Pedro knocks and enters.*) Well?

PEDRO. Dona Catarina?

CATARINA (*furious*). Dona Catarina in her dressing-gown! Just the right moment to choose for your faultless bows, for affected, secretarial phrases. The devil take you if you don't speak to the point.

PEDRO (*confused*). But what about, Dona Catarina?

CATARINA. About the lilies, about the roses! Pedro, I am being deceived.

PEDRO. Deceived, madam?

ROSITA. We're speaking of the cup.

CATARINA. For ten years I've been living in a state of delusion, and no one tells me.

PEDRO. Dona Catarina, it happened about seven years ago. The tray slipped out of the maid's hands.

CATARINA (*sharply*). We are speaking of the tenth of June, 1580, that is, rather more than ten years ago.

ROSITA. You even know the date! So you must have known, too, that I brought you the lily pattern every morning.

CATARINA. That morning, so they said, Luiz Vaz de Camoens died of the plague in Lisbon. Pedro, reflect on it, think of the delusions under which I live; and no one bothers to dispel them.

PEDRO. Dona Catarina, do you doubt for a moment –

CATARINA. Who said anything about doubts? Fetch some red wine, Rosita.

ROSITA. Before sundown?

CATARINA. This is an unusual day.

ROSITA. Very well, madam.

(*Exit Rosita.*)

CATARINA. Certainly, Pedro, that's it. The pattern on the cup has opened my eyes. How blindly we live on from day to day. Merely because we never ask anyone.

PEDRO. Dona Catarina, even if you ask me –

CATARINA. It's too late now, Pedro, you can't deceive

me now. Sit down. We must discuss the details.

PEDRO. The pattern seemed insignificant to me.

CATARINA. As insignificant as the plague of which Camoens died. The details of the journey, Pedro!

PEDRO. But the King commanded you never to leave Setúbal.

CATARINA. Ten years lost, and you want me to lose more time? I know that Camoens is alive, and I am going to see him.

PEDRO. Who's alive? See whom?

CATARINA. I believed in his death as I believed in the rose pattern. We are leaving for Lisbon.

On the terrace of Catarina's house.

PEDRO. At first I thought that this journey didn't fit in with our plans. But after a little reflection –

ROSITA. A good thing that you reflect. Personally I've given it up. Everything seems to black out when I start thinking. How can you bear it?

PEDRO. Bear it? What has that got to do with thinking? A man has to make decisions, hasn't he?

ROSITA. All right, you can take on the decisions. As for me, I'll take on the black-outs for you.

PEDRO. Don't be silly. Has Dona Catarina enough red wine?

ROSITA. Two litres. If that isn't enough, she'll ring.

PEDRO. I shall make it clear to her that we need a second coach. This journey is a stroke of luck for us. Like this we can even take things that would have been a great hindrance otherwise, things like the china, the heavy silver –

ROSITA. Oh, Pedro –

PEDRO. What?

ROSITA. The prospect of committing a theft is like a great expectation. I never thought that one day I may really be looking back on it.

PEDRO. Theft, you say? It's more than that. It's the whole matter of our life together, Rosita, and don't you forget it.

ROSITA. I don't forget it; but my conscience –

PEDRO. It would give me a bad conscience to leave such a lot of money and property in the hands of a madwoman. What does she need, after all! Red wine, bread and a bit of rolling sea.

ROSITA. Is she really mad? Listen, Pedro, the window is open, but can you hear anything?

PEDRO. What do you expect me to hear?

ROSITA. The rolling sea. Be quiet!

(*Pause*)

PEDRO. I can't hear anything.

ROSITA. That's just what I mean. I don't hear anything either. But she can hear it.

PEDRO. That's what proves that she's mad. She can hear the rolling sea, and is going off to Lisbon to visit a dead man.

ROSITA. I've never troubled to think whether he's alive or dead. But why shouldn't he be alive? Did anyone see him die?

PEDRO. He may be alive, for all I care. In that case he'll be enchanted to see his lovely Natercia again as an old hag smelling of red wine. Whether he's alive or dead, he gives us the opportunity to go to Lisbon and take possession of the treasures in this house. I'm ready to raise my hat to him or to

shed a tear over his grave. In either case he'll help
us to attain prosperity, and to do it soon, Rosita.

ROSITA. Rosita –

PEDRO. What do you mean?

ROSITA. Couldn't you perhaps call me by a different
name for a change?

PEDRO. What different name? Don't you like the one
you have?

ROSITA. All I mean is a different name.

PEDRO. For instance?

ROSITA. For instance: Natercia.

PEDRO. Natercia! (*He bursts out laughing.*)

ROSITA. I only gave it as an instance. I know the name
sounds silly.

PEDRO. Then why –

ROSITA. But I should have been glad all the same if
you'd called me that.

PEDRO. Natercia.

ROSITA. That or a different name.

PEDRO. Antonia, Inez, Esther, Francisca, Margarida,
Maria –

ROSITA. Now it doesn't count any more.

PEDRO. Enough of these stupidities. You're too sentimental.

ROSITA. I'm not sentimental. I was only joking.
(*A ring.*)

PEDRO. It's the old girl.

ROSITA. And now I'm going to indulge in the joke of
telling her that we intend to rob her.

PEDRO. Are you mad?

ROSITA. I have my duties towards Dona Catarina.
What she expects of me is not only the chocolate
and the red wine, but some sweetmeat to go with

it. The customs officer's love affairs are her Madeira cake, stories about the bishop her macaroons. She eats too much sweet stuff.

PEDRO. Rosita, do you mean to say you're going to –

(*Another ring.*)

ROSITA. Something savoury, Pedro, a few cheese straws –

(*She runs up the stairs.*)

PEDRO (*calls after her*). Rosita!

ROSITA (*knocks on Dona Catarina's door and enters*). A little more wine, Dona Catarina?

CATARINA. There's enough left for a conversation with you. Sit on my bed.

ROSITA. Do you hear the rolling sea, Dona Catarina?

CATARINA. Of course. Altogether it's a fact that I've heard it more clearly since my hearing began to get weak. But what was I going to say to you?

ROSITA. Something about the journey perhaps?

CATARINA (*thoughtful*). Yes, of course, that was it.

ROSITA. Or shall I tell you something? I know of something.

CATARINA. Fancy that.

ROSITA. You see, Pedro and I have got together –

CATARINA. You mustn't think I haven't noticed that. I've always had a subtle flair for the first stirrings of love.

ROSITA. Got together to rob you of all your wealth. We intend to make use of the journey to Lisbon to take possession of all your property.

CATARINA (*laughing*). That's a good one.

ROSITA. Not only good, but true.

CATARINA. I can see through you, rascals that you are.

ROSITA. How do you mean that, Dona Catarina?

CATARINA. Just another attempt to prevent the journey. Admit it, Rosita.

ROSITA. I admit everything.

CATARINA. First you say the coach is too small, then the horses go lame, then the wheel is broken, then we have no money, and now you're going to rob me. If I weren't fond of you, I should be angry with you for this. Why are you taking part in the conspiracy against me?

ROSITA. What conspiracy?

CATARINA. Do you think I haven't noticed it? No matter, though, not another word about it. And not another word from you to keep me from going to Lisbon. Go ahead and rob me, you miserable little thieves, go ahead and rob me! (*She laughs.*)

In the open. The coach approaches at walking speed and stops.

PEDRO. The Golden Key, Dona Catarina.

CATARINA. So this is where it was. But the house is painted black. Was it at that time too?

ROSITA. An inn with black distemper on the walls? It's unbelievable. No, Dona Catarina, it's a coffin. Let's move on.

CATARINA. The golden sign goes well with it.

ROSITA. Coffins too have golden metal-work on them if I remember rightly.

CATARINA. And the window-frames are white – it's in good taste, whatever else it may be. No objections please, my timid little dove! It's part of our itinerary to spend the night here. Hey there landlord! (*To Pedro*) Is it the same man as before?

PEDRO. He certainly wasn't as bent as that. I suppose it's because of his noble guests, who drag a man's head down to the ground.

LANDLORD (*approaching*). At your service, Your Grace, it's due to the passage of time, if I may take the liberty of having overheard. You have stopped at the Golden Key, as the sign tells you. The Golden Key, so the legend has it –

PEDRO. Thank you; we are looking for lodgings suitable for a lady.

LANDLORD. Look no further, then. Even if my rooms were bad, they're the only ones between Setúbal and Lisbon.

PEDRO. So the rooms are bad?

CATARINA. I remember now.

LANDLORD. I used the subjunctive.

CATARINA. It's by the subjunctive that I recognize him.

PEDRO. This is a lady of high rank with her attendants. Two coaches.

LANDLORD. So I observe. She will drown in leopard skins. We have Indian, African and Chinese rooms.

CATARINA. I remember more and more clearly. Even these words were uttered ten years ago.

LANDLORD. But ten years ago I was in the habit of adding: the windows overlook a world empire. They no longer overlook a world empire. That is why I chose black paint for the walls.

PEDRO. A patriot.

LANDLORD. It puts off a good many potential guests. But I am conscious of what I owe to my country's decline.

CATARINA. No doubt at all. It's the same man. Have

the horses unharnessed, Pedro. Support me, Rosita.

LANDLORD. Your Grace will be satisfied.

CATARINA. For that I need something different from a leopard skin. But you could make a good start by advising the fleas to practise a little reticence.

LANDLORD. I shall pass on your order. And what else can I do for Your Grace?

CATARINA. Red wine in my room.

LANDLORD. At your service. It is excellent. I drink it myself.

CATARINA. Then you will drink it with me. I have something to discuss with you. Where are my rooms?

LANDLORD. The whole of the first floor is at your disposal.

CATARINA. Pedro will call you.

LANDLORD. At your service.

CATARINA. It appears that you don't recognize me?

LANDLORD. I have the feeling that I know you well, though I am sure that we have not met very often.

PEDRO. A diplomatic reply.

LANDLORD. But the truth all the same.

PEDRO. We said, ten years ago.

LANDLORD (*thinking hard*). Ten years ago? That was a short time before I put on the black distemper, about the time when Camoens died.

CATARINA. Has Camoens died?

LANDLORD. Of the plague, in Lisbon. On the 10th of June 1580. I used to know him personally, went to India with him, and know his sonnets by heart –

ROSITA. No measure now is valid, but thine own,
　　　Natercia, for eternity and time –

LANDLORD. What? Do the young people know his

verses? I shall cease to be anxious for Portugal. A good reason for changing the colour of my house to pink or green.

PEDRO. Don't be in too great a hurry.

LANDLORD. As for Natercia: Soon after a lady came here – (*he falters*) – a lady –

PEDRO. Natercia?

LANDLORD. Yes, indeed: Natercia. (*Deferential*) As I said, madam: I am entirely at your disposal.

CATARINA. Come, Rosita.

(*Exeunt Catarina and Rosita.*)

LANDLORD. A great day for my house. But, to be honest, somewhat confusing

PEDRO. How so?

LANDLORD. The coaches would be safest in the yard.

PEDRO. I shall see to them myself.

LANDLORD. Something foolish has been done.

PEDRO. Something foolish?

LANDLORD. Not important, but very foolish all the same. Perhaps she won't notice.

PEDRO. May I know what it is?

LANDLORD. Hm.

PEDRO. Whatever it is, you may be sure that she'll ask a great many questions.

LANDLORD. I shall have it put right beforehand. I must hurry.

PEDRO (*calls after him*). That's a fine way to behave – (*grumpily to himself*) to arouse a man's curiosity and then run away. Sometimes one would think that there's nothing but madmen in the world. The only one here who knows what he's doing is myself. Gee up!

(*The coach rumbles off into the yard.*)

23

Room in the inn.

CATARINA. If you can recall it, I occupied this very room.

LANDLORD. I beg your pardon, madam, but I don't remember the details. Yet I can truthfully say that your visit itself was unforgettable.

CATARINA. It is the details that would interest me.

LANDLORD. You turned back because the plague was sweeping Lisbon.

CATARINA. That's wrong for a start: I turned back because I was informed that Camoens had died.

LANDLORD. For that reason also. You had two reasons for turning back.

CATARINA. There's no such thing; it was one reason or two excuses.

LANDLORD. That seems too peremptory to me. Our acquaintance with the poets teaches us to appreciate the finer shades – don't you think, Dona Catarina?

CATARINA. The finer shades derive from good society. Poets who startle no one are good for nothing but to provide topics for conversation.

LANDLORD. You are anticipating – by three centuries, Dona Catarina. Let us remain where we are.

CATARINA. But only for one night at the Golden Key. I am on my way to Lisbon, to visit Luis Vaz de Camoens.

LANDLORD. Luis Vaz de Camoens.

CATARINA. That's a repetition; I expect an answer.

LANDLORD. If I may permit myself a correction: you are on your way to Lisbon to visit a grave.

CATARINA. So you won't admit it?

LANDLORD. What should I admit?

CATARINA. That, on the other hand, is a question, and still no answer.

LANDLORD. If I only knew what you have in mind?

CATARINA. Presumably you know it quite well. Is your collar too tight?

LANDLORD. A change in the weather. I respond to it in advance. Since I went to the tropics I've been sensitive to the weather. And my rheumatism –

CATARINA. You put too little trust in the power of red wine. Where is the grave which I intend to visit?

LANDLORD. Oh, I didn't mean it as exactly as that.

CATARINA. Exactness is something one learns from the poets. Didn't you tell me at that time that you had spent months under the same roof with him? You have confused him with one of his commentators. Well, where is the grave?

LANDLORD. I thought you knew that there isn't an actual grave.

CATARINA. What is it then?

LANDLORD. Those who died of the plague were buried in a communal grave.

CATARINA. How illuminating!

LANDLORD. And even there one has to depend on guesswork. There were so many dead and no one knew him.

CATARINA. Don't you think yourself that all this, to put it mildly, is a little vague?

LANDLORD. As definite as circumstances permitted. When I was in Lisbon two years later, I questioned his servant.

CATARINA. His servant is still alive?

LANDLORD. He was alive then in any case.

CATARINA. And?

LANDLORD. I don't know why I'm telling you this.

CATARINA. The change in the weather, your rheumatism. It will rain tomorrow, isn't that so?

LANDLORD. All I am telling you I have from him, and he knew no more than what I am telling you.

CATARINA. It's all very suspicious. Every word conceals something. What's the servant's name, and where does he live?

LANDLORD. A Javanese servant, Ojao by name. At that time he lived in the Travessa da Boa Hora.

CATARINA. I expect he has died in the meantime. All the evidence is most uncertain.

LANDLORD. It's conceivable too that a man should move house.

CATARINA. People who have nothing to conceal don't move house.

LANDLORD. I no longer dare to draw your attention to the finer shades.

CATARINA. All you know derives from this servant. But already two years before you questioned him you told me that Camoens was dead. How did you know it then?

LANDLORD. Ojao confirmed what I already knew.

CATARINA. And how did you come to know it?

LANDLORD. I was told by the driver of the mail-coach, who went to Lisbon each week –

CATARINA. And what's his name?

LANDLORD. He was called Manuel Azevevo.

CATARINA. His address?

LANDLORD. He is dead; he fell off his coach box when drunk and –

CATARINA. Dead! That means that all the witnesses

are inaccessible. Oh, what a fool I was ever to have believed you! Ten years lost!

LANDLORD. Dona Catarina, there is no reason to doubt the death of the honoured –

CATARINA. Yes, there is every reason. Nor do I believe that you only gave me unreliable information. You did it on purpose.

LANDLORD. I am deeply –

CATARINA. And rightly so. But your dismay is not good enough.

LANDLORD. Yet it is more than is compatible with my self-respect.

CATARINA. Where should we be if we considered the self-respect of toads?

LANDLORD. Dona Catarina, you are making our conversation a good deal easier for me. Until now I felt obliged to conceal something from you.

CATARINA. Indeed!

LANDLORD. I gave strict instructions to my staff that not a word was to be said about it, and, above all, that the name –

CATARINA. So you are confessing it at last!

LANDLORD. Yes, I am; I confess that I have called my donkey – a jenny – Natercia.

CATARINA. That you've called your donkey –

LANDLORD. Precisely, Dona Catarina! my donkey's name is Natercia. An uncommon name, but one made familiar by the great Camoens. Don't you agree that it most aptly characterizes a stubborn attitude of mind?

CATARINA. Not really. You must have had a special reason for choosing it.

LANDLORD. If so, I wasn't aware of it till you spoke of toads.

CATARINA. Well, let me tell you the reason, then: because you were thinking of my stupidity in giving credence to you.

LANDLORD. I see that there are more possibilities than I reckoned with.

CATARINA. Do you deny it?

LANDLORD. There's something very plausible about your opinion.

CATARINA (*without paying attention to the mockery in his voice*). What prevents you from being truthful is that you're joining in the conspiracy. You're all trying to conceal the fact that he's alive. Why not admit it?

LANDLORD. Every second Thursday in the month the conspirators meet in the Golden Key. Camoens himself presides. We discuss the statutes and issue new directives. At the same time we eat and drink. You will understand that I am reluctant to forgo the profit which accrues to me from these items.

CATARINA. At first you tried what you could do by deferential readiness to serve, but I saw through you. Then I provoked you to insults, and I knew how to extract the truth even from these. Now you resort to mockery, with no more success than before. There remains one other course: see what you can do by accepting the truth for once.

LANDLORD (*with a sigh*). Your truth, Dona Catarina. But in one regard I shall submit to you: I shall call my next donkey Felipe. For that happens to be my name. Really, I'm going round in a circle and pulling a whim-chain. But there's no question of either

water or corn. It's a question of stones, Dona
Catarina, and you think that they can be made to
yield oil.

CATARINA (*almost imploring*). Why don't you stop
hedging!

LANDLORD (*sighing again*). Very well, then. What is
our reason for withholding the fact that Camoens is
alive?

CATARINA. Oh, but part of the conspiracy consists in
concealing the reason for the concealment.

LANDLORD (*somewhat exhausted*). I see.

CATARINA. Now you're beginning to understand.

LANDLORD. And for what reason does Camoens himself
withhold it from you?

CATARINA. If you can only grasp it, this very circum-
stance proves the existence of a conspiracy.

LANDLORD. No, I cannot grasp it.

CATARINA. You insist on controverting all the arguments. Do stop hedging at last, make a clean breast.

LANDLORD (*gasping*). I have, madam, I have. You may
not believe me, but it was a physical strain. It
seems that to stop hedging is to leap over an
abyss.

CATARINA. And now?

LANDLORD. Now I'm in the open; but it's a most arid
landscape.

CATARINA. Well, just pay attention for a moment,
Don Felipe.

LANDLORD (*groaning*). It's the change in the weather,
you see.

CATARINA. There is no proof at all that Camoens is dead.

LANDLORD. I admit that the information –

CATARINA. All the information is second- or third-hand. That means it's worthless. No one saw him die.

LANDLORD. True enough.

CATARINA. From that I conclude that he's alive.

LANDLORD. Certainly it is difficult to prove the contrary.

CATARINA. Didn't I tell you so!

LANDLORD. To be sure, he could be ill, perhaps incapable of communicating with you –

CATARINA. Ill, did you say? Of course. That's the explanation.

LANDLORD. Not so fast, Dona Catarina. I'm too short of breath for conclusions of that kind. I never said a word about his being ill.

CATARINA. So you think I'm deaf as well as –

LANDLORD. Dona Catarina, I'm prepared to admit anything you like. And yet my advice is: Turn back tomorrow.

CATARINA. What? You presume to suggest I should not go to Lisbon?

LANDLORD. Today it's like ten years ago, Dona Catarina. The plague is in Lisbon again, it forestalled you.

CATARINA. Well, this time the scare won't prevent me. (*Laughing*) The plague, a dangerous illness, what! A marvellous illness to prevent someone from going on a journey! An illness of which Camoens has already died! The plague, Don Felipe, is an invention. There's no such thing as the plague, either in Lisbon or anywhere else. There never was such a thing! You may as well give up trying, for you won't deceive me again. (*Laughing more and*

more loudly) The plague, the plague, who ever heard –
   (*Fade out.*)

In the ante-room.

ROSITA. The plague, Pedro, the plague!

PEDRO. I heard it, Rosita. Now get away from the keyhole.

ROSITA. We must talk her out of it, Pedro.

PEDRO. She doesn't suspect the least thing. There's no danger.

ROSITA. No danger, you say?

PEDRO. Go in and tell her that I've hidden her jewels under the coach-box. Her confidence in me will be all the greater.

ROSITA. But what about the hundreds, the thousands of people who've died of the plague?

PEDRO. Oh, but think of how many have *not* died of the plague.

ROSITA. Be sensible, Pedro.

PEDRO. Be sensible, Rosita.

ROSITA. We must turn back.

PEDRO. Tell Dona Catarina, then.

ROSITA. No, even if she won't.

PEDRO. We shall go to Lisbon, even if she refuses to go. The matter is settled.

ROSITA. But if the circumstances demand –

PEDRO. I'm not a crab.

ROSITA. There's such a thing as a wrong decision.

PEDRO. Enough of that. The thought of spending a night sitting up in the coach is bad enough –

ROSITA. What a ridiculous precaution!

PEDRO. All the same; those gold coins weigh on me. That's a pleasing thought, displeasing though it may be. The plague, on the other hand –

ROSITA. I'm quite sure that in Lisbon you'll look very carefully at your finger-tips.

PEDRO. The plague is an invention of landlords, as Dona Catarina very rightly observed. Altogether her arguments are a great deal better than yours.

ROSITA. Aren't you worried on my account?

PEDRO. One's first worry is always for oneself. That shows you how sure I am.

ROSITA. A pity.

PEDRO. It was a pity that I didn't call you Natercia. Oh, my dear little jenny – when the night will be hard enough for me, why do you try to spoil the day as well? Think of our future, of our wealth –

ROSITA. I think of it continually, and can never help thinking of Dona Catarina's poverty at the same time.

PEDRO. Quite correct. One follows from the other. But don't forget that she'll have her red wine still, and an inexhaustible store of dreams.

ROSITA. I don't think her dreams are pleasant ones. You know how often she screams, how often she wakes me up –

PEDRO. And how often you have to call me. The devil take her if she doesn't leave us in peace tonight.

Dona Catarina's bedroom at the Golden Key.

CATARINA. Rosita, Rosita! Extraordinary how these young things can sleep! No wonder her intelligence is deficient. Rosita!

ROSITA. Madam?

CATARINA. You forgot to open the window.

ROSITA. It is open, Dona Catarina.

CATARINA. Then why don't I hear the rolling sea?

ROSITA. Because we are not at Setúbal.

CATARINA. That's not a good reason, but still –

ROSITA. But what?

CATARINA. My dressing-gown, and help me out of bed.

ROSITA. It must be about three o'clock.

CATARINA. A good time of day.

ROSITA. For what?

CATARINA. For thieves. Didn't you know that? We shall creep through the house on stockinged feet. Come on.

(*The door opens.*)

ROSITA. Where to, Dona Catarina? And in the middle of the night?

CATARINA. Are you afraid?

ROSITA. Perhaps there's a dog in the house.

CATARINA. The door to the yard should be unlocked, don't you think?

ROSITA. Do you want to go out into the yard, Dona Catarina?

CATARINA. Just a breath of fresh air.

(*They open the door to the yard.*)

Stars, a moon. Our two coaches are well illuminated. Really they look quite imposing, quite inviting – out there in the open –

C

ROSITA. Do you think, then – you spoke of thieves a little while ago – Pedro, too, thought it was incautious to –

CATARINA. Did he think so? What would we do without Pedro? In that case I dare say it's Pedro sitting there in the coach?

ROSITA. It is.

CATARINA. Well fancy that. I thought it was a thief.

ROSITA. No, it's Pedro.

CATARINA. Shall we try to steal something? I'm sure he won't notice. He's snoring.

ROSITA. Steal something?

CATARINA. A string of pearls, a brocade gown, a bag of ducats; why, we could extract a whole fortune from under the seat, and he wouldn't notice it.

ROSITA. A pity there's no fortune under the seat.

CATARINA. Yes, you're right. It isn't worth while, especially since I have more important business to attend to here.

ROSITA. What important business could there be in this yard at three o'clock in the morning?

CATARINA. A visit, Rosita.

ROSITA. You're perfectly right: a very good hour.

CATARINA. I started up from my sleep because I neglected all the proprieties. Isn't it proper to call on one's namesake?

ROSITA (*giggling*). I think you're overdoing the formalities, Dona Catarina.

CATARINA. Don't laugh, you silly thing. I don't think it at all impossible that Natercia feels offended.

ROSITA. Natercia?

CATARINA. Where's the stable door?

ROSITA. Couldn't it have been you who had reason to feel offended?

CATARINA. Am I not Natercia?

ROSITA. What a lot of questions. This could be it.
(*They open the stable door, which creaks slightly.*)

CATARINA. What can you see?

ROSITA. Hens, I think. Wait till my eyes have got used to it.

CATARINA. What else?

ROSITA. Sacks of barley.

CATARINA. That sounds right. (*Listening*) Do you hear something?

ROSITA. Something is stirring in the stalls. Could it be our horses?

CATARINA. Or Don Felipe's jenny. (*She calls out softly.*) Natercia!

ROSITA (*likewise*). Natercia!

CATARINA. Natercia!

ROSITA. There's a clattering noise in the stall.

CATARINA. Natercia!
(*The donkey utters a piercing cry.*)

CATARINA. That's enough, Rosita. Let's go.

ROSITA. Goodness, what a fright that animal gave me.
(*She closes the stable door.*)

CATARINA. It was a plain answer.

ROSITA. You're looking pale, Dona Catarina.

CATARINA. It's the moon, Rosita.

ROSITA. You're shivering.

CATARINA. Sometimes the nights are cool.

ROSITA. Yes.

CATARINA. I hope it hasn't woken our friend Pedro.

ROSITA. I don't suppose that would matter much.

CATARINA. What did you think of when the donkey cried?

ROSITA. Nothing. It made me jump.

CATARINA. Nor did I think of anything. It startled me too.

ROSITA. We should go to bed.

CATARINA. But when I heard that cry I suddenly knew that we're all going to die.

ROSITA (*constrained*). There's nothing new about that.

CATARINA. No, but I've only just discovered it.

ROSITA. Of course we're all going to die.

CATARINA. Yes, even the one over there, in the coach.

(*A pause. Then the coach starts, the horses trot, the whip cracks. The sounds fade.*)

A narrow room.

OJAO. It was about six o'clock in the morning, and I went to the harbour to buy cod.

CATARINA. You again; but I want to know what *he* did. On the 10th of June 1580; you know which day I mean.

OJAO. The cod is not without importance either. Do you never take lunch, madam?

CATARINA. We are now at six o'clock in the morning.

OJAO. I have already said so. And that morning it was the bells that said so.

CATARINA. Six o'clock is not the only time the bells peal.

OJAO. True enough. A noisy religion, this one to which I've been converted! Bells and cannonades. I come from Java, Dona Catarina.

CATARINA. Firstly, you're a bad Christian. Secondly, Java is too far a digression. What did Don Luis say when you went out?

OJAO. He said nothing.

CATARINA. Was he still asleep?

OJAO. He was not asleep, nor was he awake.

CATARINA. Rosita, here you see someone capable of answering questions even more badly than you do.

ROSITA. In that case Don Luis shared your fate in many ways, Dona Catarina.

CATARINA. Where did you get that from, Rosita? These young people! They've hardly reached the capital, and here they are rattling it off like the natives. Well, what didn't Don Luis say, then?

OJAO. He groaned. I made him some tea out of magnolia leaves.

ROSITA. Magnolia?

OJAO. Leaves. A recipe from Java.

ROSITA. That most certainly could do him no good. Where is this place, Java?

OJAO. It's a country – oh, palm trees, the odour of cinnamon.

CATARINA. Stop! Stop! We are talking of Don Luis.

OJAO. I was with him for ten years. I lay beside him on the decks of ships, on the bare boards, when the sails were tattered. At receptions I kept my distance, in the prisons I was close to him. I washed his clothes, cleaned his shoes, I –

CATARINA. And what did you do on that day?

OJAO. When he had drunk a little – he found it difficult to swallow – I put down the jug near the straw.

CATARINA. What straw?

OJAO. Near the straw on which he lay.

ROSITA. A Javanese custom?

OJAO. Not exclusively Javanese. Practised wherever there is poverty and straw.

CATARINA. Poverty?

OJAO. The poverty had come of itself. As for the straw, I had stolen it from the royal stables, and picked the magnolias on the river-banks – and I would obtain our fish by begging around the harbour.

CATARINA. What did I eat on the 10th of June 1580?

ROSITA. I wasn't in your service then.

CATARINA. How fortunate! Then I can say that I was fasting.

OJAO. I had to go there at six in the morning, for that was the most favourable hour. At that time I was likely to meet a fisherman who valued the poems of Don Luis. An uncommonly stingy fellow, unfortunately.

CATARINA. And Don Luis remained all alone?

OJAO. The people in the house passed by from time to time, on their way to the cellar. We were living in a recess under the cellar stairs. When I went out –

CATARINA. At six. Don Luis on the straw –

OJAO. He was quite brown already.

CATARINA. Brown?

OJAO. Dark brown. The plague.

CATARINA. And you?

OJAO. I had it in Java.

ROSITA. So there are people who don't die of it?

OJAO. Not many, but it does happen. Perhaps I was spared so as to be able to answer your questions.

CATARINA. One must bear in mind that it does happen.

OJAO. I was in luck that day. I got two cod heads. Perhaps, I thought to myself, Don Luis would eat some after all.

CATARINA. And did he?

OJAO. He died before I had cooked them.

CATARINA. Steady there, not so fast! You came back –

OJAO. He was hardly breathing.

CATARINA. Had he drunk anything?

OJAO. I think he was too weak. I moistened his lips.

CATARINA. And then you cooked the fish?

OJAO. I could see that it wasn't the right moment to cook fish. I stayed with Don Luis.

CATARINA. And – when – ?

OJAO. About an hour later.

CATARINA. That was at –

OJAO. It was about nine when I got back from the harbour. It must have happened just before ten. Soon after closing his eyes I heard the bells. And soon after that I heard the plague rattle. The cart was passing near by. I ran out and called the corpse-bearers. They put him on the cart.

CATARINA. With the others.

OJAO. With the others.

CATARINA. Where did the cart go?

OJAO. At that moment I felt sick. I vomited and then dragged myself to the cellar. There I slept till the evening.

CATARINA. Do you mean to say you didn't see where Don Luis was buried?

OJAO. No, but he died in my arms.

CATARINA. So I've been told already. The strange thing, however, is that he did not die at all.

OJAO. What?

39

CATARINA. You heard what I said. Don Luis is alive. How could he be, when he died in your arms? Or is it possible that you were mistaken?

OJAO (*confused*). Could I have been mistaken? But where is Don Luis? Why doesn't he come?

CATARINA. Could you have been mistaken?

OJAO. If he's alive, I may have made a mistake. Let him come.

CATARINA. He will come when we know the truth.

OJAO. I wasn't so difficult. I went to Portugal with him. A strange country, to put it mildly, and I don't believe that it contains more truth than Java. Why does he hide from me?

CATARINA. Yes, why does he?

OJAO (*pensive*). If he's still alive, he could be either with you –

CATARINA. Or else?

OJAO. Or else at his mother's.

CATARINA. At his mother's?

OJAO. Yet it would be extraordinary if she'd been able to conceal it from me. Very little that happens in this district is concealed from me for long.

CATARINA. So she lives in the same district? I didn't know she was still alive.

OJAO. She is eighty, perhaps even ninety.

CATARINA. But since he died in your arms, how can you assume that he's at his mother's?

OJAO. It was you who said he's alive.

CATARINA. So you must have made a mistake. Admit it.

OJAO. One is reluctant to retract an assertion which one has repeated for ten years. Nevertheless, for Don Luis –

CATARINA. It is honourable to admit an error.

OJAO. But is it honourable, too, to admit a lie?

CATARINA. A lie?

OJAO. Don Luis will forgive me. For if you take it all too literally, he didn't die in my arms. He was still alive when I went to the harbour, that much is certain.

CATARINA. And when you returned?

OJAO. When I returned? I must add that I was a little late.

CATARINA. A little? When did you return?

OJAO. I met a girl, and we ate fish together. It must have been the early afternoon.

CATARINA. Not before the evening, you mean!

OJAO. I admit that it was growing dark.

CATARINA. And when you got back he was dead?

OJAO. He was neither alive nor dead. He was gone.

CATARINA. Gone? Gone out?

OJAO. They said he had died towards noon, and the plague cart had removed him. But it's possible too –

CATARINA. What's possible?

OJAO. You can imagine that people don't like to think that there's a man sick of the plague in their house. So it's possible, too –

CATARINA. That they had him removed before –

OJAO. That is the possibility which your words suggest to me.

ROSITA. Only a few more questions, and you will have brought him back to life, Dona Catarina.

CATARINA. Now to his mother's. Lead us there, Ojao.
(*Pause*)

Another room.

MOTHER. Dona Catarina de Ataide. Yes, I know your name. You brought my son no luck.

CATARINA. Does he say so? I should have thought –

MOTHER. I say so. But the young people are so high-spirited, they don't know what to do with themselves. A capricious person. Red-haired, are you not?

CATARINA. Fair.

OJAO. Where does this door lead, Dona Antonia?

MOTHER. Where should it lead, imbecile? Into the underworld, otherwise known as the cellar.

OJAO. Why did you say underworld?

CATARINA. Yes, that's suspicious.

OJAO. It's behind that door we should look, isn't it, Dona Antonia?

MOTHER. Of course it is. Where else would it be?

OJAO. We've got him.

ROSITA. The cellar is what Dona Antonia means.

MOTHER. What are you chattering about? You must raise your voices.

CATARINA. Does Don Luis come to see you every day, Dona Antonia?

MOTHER. Without fail.

CATARINA. Does he live with you?

MOTHER. It seems as though he lived with me and as though he were still alive. We discuss everything. He told me that he had to keep away from Court because of you, Dona Catarina. Why were you at Court?

ROSITA. Dona Catarina was lady-in-waiting to Her Majesty the Queen.

MOTHER (*tenderly*). He was a ne'er-do-well, that Luis. Later he wrote verses.

ROSITA. Even at that time he did. Natercia –

CATARINA. Hold your tongue. (*To the mother*) I should like to speak to Don Luis too.

MOTHER. Then he fought a duel, also because of you. You're responsible for everything. India, China, Madagascar, a musket shot in his left eye, prison, exile – it's all your fault. If only I could see better – I should really like to take a good look at this red-haired person who was the ruin of him. Step closer, my daughter.

CATARINA (*mumbling*). Don't imagine I haven't suffered. Twenty-seven years of Setúbal –

MOTHER. Oh yes, I can imagine it now. The pretty masks women wear when they're young!

CATARINA. So you see me with his eyes?

MOTHER. Yes, I see you with his eyes.

CATARINA. It's true, isn't it? He still lives.

MOTHER. He will live for ever, my daughter.

OJAO. Come, Dona Catarina. He's behind this door.

MOTHER. Where are you going? It's pitch-black down there. Are you going to count my cabbages?

(*Ojao and Dona Catarina go down to the cellar.*)

MOTHER. Now I want you to talk. You seem to be the most sensible of the three.

ROSITA. I'm Dona Catarina's lady's maid.

MOTHER. What do those two want in my cellar?

ROSITA. They're looking for Don Luis.

MOTHER (*happy*). Well, as it happens, he really is in the cellar.

ROSITA. So Dona Catarina is right after all. I should never have thought so

43

MOTHER. But they won't find him.

ROSITA. He must be clever at hiding.

MOTHER. He's not hiding at all. But if they didn't see him up here, they won't see him down there either.

ROSITA. Was he up here, then, all the time?

MOTHER. Certainly. Didn't he talk to you all?

ROSITA. I didn't hear anything.

MOTHER. He was sitting next to me, on this stool.

ROSITA. Oh?

MOTHER. Naturally he wasn't sitting on the stool either, but on the bench.

ROSITA. And at the same time he was in the cellar?

MOTHER. At last you've seen what I mean.

ROSITA. Not quite. I should like to know whether my poor mistress –

MOTHER. She will see him, never worry.

(*Ojao and Dona Catarina return.*)

MOTHER (*cheerfully*). Well?

CATARINA. It's uncommonly dark down there.

MOTHER. Didn't I tell you?

OJAO. But light enough to see –

ROSITA. See what?

MOTHER. My son, perhaps? Is he down there?

OJAO. Nothing. Dona Catarina, what was the use of admitting my lie?

CATARINA. It was so dark that I learned to understand darkness.

MOTHER. An excellent thing!

CATARINA. Come on, Rosita. The old woman is mocking us, and I know why.

MOTHER. Since I'm not mocking anyone, you can hardly know why.

CATARINA. The truth is I'm too old, too ugly for him.

44

The cellar has a door that leads outside. He is running away from me. He is hiding from me. Now everything is clear to me, Rosita. He himself is at the heart of the conspiracy. He himself made sure that I should receive the news that he is dead; it was he himself.

ROSITA. He himself?

CATARINA. Let's go, Rosita.

Another room.

LORD CHAMBERLAIN. Dona Catarina de Ataide.

CATARINA. Yes, I'm coming.

LORD CHAMBERLAIN. His Majesty regrets that he cannot receive you.

CATARINA. The matter is of great importance.

LORD CHAMBERLAIN. If it were not, you would not have requested an audience.

CATARINA. That is so.

LORD CHAMBERLAIN. His Majesty regrets –

CATARINA. So you said. Tomorrow perhaps?

LORD CHAMBERLAIN. You might try tomorrow.

(*A pause.*)

The scene changes.

CATARINA. Dona Catarina de Ataide requests an audience.

LORD CHAMBERLAIN. His Majesty regrets –

CATARINA. I made the same request yesterday. His Majesty appears not to remember that my family is among the most prominent in the country.

LORD CHAMBERLAIN. His Majesty does remember, but nevertheless regrets –

CATARINA. So you said.

LORD CHAMBERLAIN. Perhaps tomorrow.

CATARINA. The matter in question, you see, is my banishment.

LORD CHAMBERLAIN. Very well.

CATARINA. Nearly thirty years ago now, I was forbidden to return to Lisbon.

LORD CHAMBERLAIN. But now you have returned.

CATARINA. To beg the King –

LORD CHAMBERLAIN. You were right to return, and could have done so twenty years sooner.

CATARINA. No one told me anything about that.

LORD CHAMBERLAIN. Because your banishment was forgotten about long ago.

CATARINA. Unfortunately I did not forget it. I took the King's word to be a royal word.

LORD CHAMBERLAIN. Did I say anything to the contrary?

CATARINA. Yes, you did.

LORD CHAMBERLAIN. A misunderstanding, Dona Catarina. Well, however that may be, you can rely on me. The King will revoke your banishment.

CATARINA. You have overlooked that I myself have already revoked it.

LORD CHAMBERLAIN. But it was not your intention to –

CATARINA. The request I now have to make is a different one.

LORD CHAMBERLAIN. Would you not perhaps confide – ? My position naturally places me close to the King.

CATARINA. To you? (*Hesitant*) The fact is –

LORD CHAMBERLAIN (*encouragingly*). Do proceed.

CATARINA. When I was banished thirty years ago, I was still young.

LORD CHAMBERLAIN. If it is any consolation to you, Dona Catarina, none of us has grown any younger during these thirty years.

CATARINA. It is no consolation to me. For I was not only young – I was beautiful.

LORD CHAMBERLAIN. Dona Catarina, I can see it still.

CATARINA. But Don Luis Vaz de Camoens does not see it.

LORD CHAMBERLAIN. Camoens? The poet?

CATARINA. He avoids meeting me.

LORD CHAMBERLAIN. I was under the impression that he is dead.

CATARINA. Mere rumours! I know the truth.

LORD CHAMBERLAIN. Well, maybe. And I happen to have little interest in poetry. Personally I collect butterflies.

CATARINA. And now I wanted to beg the King, since he banished me and took away thirty years of my life – it was all at his command, you see.

LORD CHAMBERLAIN. I do see.

CATARINA. I wanted to beg the King to give me back my beauty.

LORD CHAMBERLAIN. To give you back your beauty?

CATARINA. Yes.

LORD CHAMBERLAIN (*reflective*). Beauty. That, certainly, is something which only the King himself can decide.

CATARINA. Yes, I thought so too. That's why I presumed that an audience –

LORD CHAMBERLAIN. Very well, I shall see.

CATARINA. Perhaps tomorrow?

LORD CHAMBERLAIN. Yes. You might try tomorrow.

(*A pause.*)

The scene changes.

CATARINA. Dona Catarina de Ataide begged His Majesty for an audience – but I assume that today also His Majesty regrets –

LORD CHAMBERLAIN. Oh no, Dona Catarina.

CATARINA. You mean I can see the King?

LORD CHAMBERLAIN. I beg you to follow me, Dona Catarina. I am taking you to the throne-room.

(*They go through doors, along passages and stairs.*)

CATARINA. It's all been rebuilt. But for you, I shouldn't have found my way any more. Or perhaps it's simply too long ago.

LORD CHAMBERLAIN. Most probably it's simply too long ago.

(*They stop.*)

LORD CHAMBERLAIN. The throne-room, Dona Catarina.

(*He opens a door.*)

CATARINA. But –

LORD CHAMBERLAIN. What were you going to say Dona Catarina?

CATARINA. That is no throne – that's a coffin!

LORD CHAMBERLAIN. His Majesty the King died early this morning of the plague.

(*Outside bells begin to ring. They come to a crescendo.*)

The scene changes to the open air.

ROSITA. Dona Catarina, did you speak to the King?

CATARINA. He was very gracious, Rosita. Where's Pedro, where's the coach?

ROSITA. I'm glad you spoke to the King. Because, you see –

CATARINA. What?

ROSITA. I mean, in that case perhaps it won't be quite so bad.

CATARINA. What won't be?

ROSITA. You see, Dona Catarina, there isn't a coach any more, and no Pedro.

CATARINA. But you're still here.

ROSITA. Yes, I'm still here.

CATARINA. We shall have to go on foot.

ROSITA. Yes.

CATARINA. I am very glad that you are still here. Don't worry about it. If we want to return to Setúbal, it's really a good thing to be rid of all that troublesome luggage.

ROSITA. If you look at it that way, Dona Catarina –

CATARINA. That's the way I look at it.

(*A pause.*)

In the open air – on the ferry.

CATARINA. Farewell, Lisbon, hill above the Tejo –

ROSITA. A good day for our crossing, plenty of wind in the sails.

CATARINA. And the dolphins are playing. One would so much like to see a connection between the

D

weather and the leave-taking. Farewell, Lisbon.

ROSITA. The sky so blue!

CATARINA. The sky blue or grey – every colour doubles the pain. I know it, Rosita: the weather itself is a kind of leave-taking. Why don't you wave?

ROSITA. Whom should I wave to?

CATARINA. To the sky, the dolphins, the children on the shore. But you don't wave because you're hiding your hands.

ROSITA. Why should I be hiding my hands?

CATARINA. The King's face was black as he lay on his catafalque. I don't think they will lay him out in the Cathedral. But I'm not thinking of the King, I'm thinking of you. I noticed that you're looking at your finger-tips in secret.

ROSITA. You must have made a mistake, Dona Catarina. I am not looking at my fingers – I'm not afraid.

CATARINA. And neither should you be. I gathered that this time far fewer people died than ten years ago.

ROSITA. Yes, it isn't so bad this time.

CATARINA. Show me your hands.

ROSITA. There you are: as white as could be!

CATARINA. True enough, as white as could be. It's hardly credible.

ROSITA. Why, didn't you expect them to be?

CATARINA. Of course I did.

ROSITA (*laughing*). And your hands, Dona Catarina?

CATARINA. Quiet, girl – so that the crew won't throw me overboard at this stage – so near the shore.

ROSITA. Why – ?

CATARINA. Isn't it enough that I don't show them to you, Rosita?

ROSITA. I understand.

CATARINA. But believe me if I tell you that I didn't notice it till we were on the ferry. Or I should never have asked you to come with me.

ROSITA. It doesn't matter, Dona Catarina.

CATARINA. Turn back; take the same boat back.

ROSITA. Where to?

CATARINA. To Pedro. It would be a comfort to me to know that you are provided for.

ROSITA. It would be no comfort to me. You see, Dona Catarina, I ceased to be afraid of the plague when I found out that it exists.

CATARINA. You'll have to repeat that at some other time. I believe it's the sentence in which the world begins for me. Anyway, it's a royal plague; I touched the purple on the coffin.

ROSITA. In that case I can assume that, for reasons of rank alone, the plague will pass me by.

CATARINA. Nevertheless I order you always to keep at a distance of three paces. One can't be sure that the aristocratic distinctions are universally observed.

(*The ship's bell rings. Fade out.*)

At the Golden Key.

LANDLORD. Wife, wife!

WIFE. No need to shout so loud. I'm no more asleep than you are.

LANDLORD. And in your case it isn't the weather. What is it, then?

WIFE. It's the moon, because it shines so brightly into

the room. Or else the dogs in the distance. And the animals too are stirring in the stable, rattling their chains. And why aren't you asleep?

LANDLORD. I was just thinking how the Golden Key is falling to pieces. It's hardly worth carrying on.

WIFE. Soon the white distemper will show through again through the black. That will be an advantage in some ways.

LANDLORD. And then I was thinking what I should say when I'm questioned at the Last Judgment. There's so little solid evidence one can present.

WIFE. Well, there's time enough to think about that. Besides, they're unlikely to ask about the Golden Key of all things. An inn counts about as much and as little as a feeding trough or the royal sceptre.

LANDLORD. I know that. And I'm not talking about ultimate values.

WIFE. What are you talking about, then?

LANDLORD. My rheumatism. Wife, it isn't the rain that I feel in my bones, it's the angels and their swords.

WIFE. Don't trouble your head about it, Felipe – it all comes of your mixing with poets.

LANDLORD. Can't you hear it?

WIFE. The last trumpet, I suppose.

LANDLORD. No, someone clapping his hands. Quiet!

WIFE. I hear something too.

LANDLORD. Let's get up and light up the house. I knew it would come tonight.

WIFE. It's your addiction to dramatic effects, Felipe. What's coming tonight?

LANDLORD. My rheumatism. And later, perhaps, some guests.

WIFE. What about opening the window?

LANDLORD. A good idea. (*He opens the window and calls out.*) Hallo?

ROSITA (*outside*). Don Felipe! Landlord!

LANDLORD. Who is it? (*Softly, to his wife*) Two women.

ROSITA. Dona Catarina and her maid.

LANDLORD. Ah! One moment, please. I'm coming down. Where's your coach?

ROSITA. We've come on foot.

WIFE. Ladies, and travelling on foot. Did you hear that?

ROSITA. Dona Catarina's feet are sore with walking, and she can't go any further.

LANDLORD. In that case she must be got to bed.

WIFE. And it's time, too. Long past midnight.

ROSITA. We must hurry, landlord, we must get to Setúbal. The rolling sea is waiting for Dona Catarina.

LANDLORD. The rolling sea will wait till tomorrow. (*To his wife*) This confirms my premonitions. It's a night full of arthritis. (*Loudly, out of the window*) What news of the plague in Lisbon?

ROSITA. The King has died.

LANDLORD. So that's it.

CATARINA. Nonsense, Rosita. Tell him the truth.

LANDLORD. Is that you, Dona Catarina?

CATARINA. Camoens died ten years ago of the plague.

LANDLORD. Oh, are you sure?

CATARINA. Quite sure.

ROSITA. Dona Catarina is not accustomed to walking barefoot. For the sake of God's mercy, saddle a donkey for us.

WIFE. Tell them: Not for God's mercy, but for Portuguese ducats. (*To herself*) The King has died. I believe he was a fool. Who would his successor be?

LANDLORD. He was childless.

WIFE. Trust him to be that.

LANDLORD. Just as we are.

WIFE. What about the donkey?

LANDLORD. Hm.

WIFE. Saddle Natercia for them. It will be the ruin of us, but perhaps it will help your arthritis.

(*A door opens and shuts.*)

ROSITA (*down below*). Are you still there, Don Felipe?

WIFE (*calls down*). He's gone to the stable. Be patient.

In the open air.

ROSITA. All will be well, Dona Catarina.

CATARINA. Our religion tells us that. No need for you to repeat it. And in our specific case: all *is* well already.

ROSITA. How so?

CATARINA. The moon is bright enough to show me how you are melting with pity. How foolish! Forgive me for telling you so, Rosita.

ROSITA. Tell me everything.

CATARINA. If only one could! You're always inclined to exaggerate, my child. No, it's much simpler than that: since I've had the plague I've known that the plague exists. And since the plague exists, the other exists no less.

ROSITA. The other?

CATARINA. Don't pretend that you don't understand. You understand much more than you are aware. Didn't you say: I ceased to be afraid of the plague when I found out that it exists.

ROSITA. I did.

CATARINA. Since it's true that Camoens died, it's also true that he desired me. His love is the truth, and the plague has given it back to me. What a fine circle it is, worthy of the orbits of the sun and moon. Look at me, Rosita: the plague has given me back my youth. Thanks to the King.

ROSITA. Yes, Dona Catarina.

CATARINA. If it's a good beast, we can be in Setúbal by daybreak. And the rolling sea can be heard some way off.

ROSITA. A long way off.

(*The stable door is opened.*)

LANDLORD. Get along, Natercia.

ROSITA. No closer, Don Felipe.

LANDLORD. I told you, Dona Catarina, didn't I? I told you the plague was in Lisbon.

CATARINA. Thank you, Don Felipe; thank you.

ROSITA. Come along, Natercia.

LANDLORD. On the left you will find a wineskin, on the right some bread, goat cheese and dates. (*The donkey breaks into a trot.*) I hope you will get home safely.

CATARINA. Thank you, Don Felipe; thank you.

(*The donkey's hoof-beats fade.*)

The Year
Lacertis

VOICES

PAUL

LAPARTE

BAYARD

KINGSLEY

ZEEMANS

RICHARDS

OLIVEIRA

MANUELA

THE OTHER MANUELA

PAUL (*narrating*). The palm trees in front of the alms-house form a dense grille, bringing human footsteps, like time, to a stop. Is it twenty years ago, or thirty? Perhaps I could work it out if I made the effort – the crosses on the burial mound would help, even where the inscriptions have been washed away by the rain or covered by the rank creepers. What has time become? The colour of a briar rose and the glitter of a snakeskin.

So I don't even know the number of the year that preceded it all. Perhaps it was 1880, but in my recollections I have called it Lacertis, a word that had meaning for me at that time although it makes no sense and I knew that it wasn't the right word.

I heard the right word on New Year's night of that same year, and I heard it in my sleep. I was lying in a ground-floor room and the window was not quite shut behind the curtains. The sound of drunks walking home and the striking of the clock on St Paul's penetrated my dream. It was shortly after six. I started when I heard the word. Someone who was passing my window must have spoken it, in conversation and by the way, though it was the word that unravelled all mysteries. While it rang out the world was transformed and comprehended, but it was no sooner uttered than forgotten. I leapt out of bed and rushed to the window. A man and a woman were walking towards the main street. Both wore black coats, the man a silk hat, the woman, who was almost as tall, something small and fashionable. It seemed that both were a bit unsteady. Were they laughing too? I called out, but they didn't turn their heads and disappeared round the corner of Fisher Street. I dressed as fast as I could and ran out in the hope of catching up with them. Thick snowflakes fell on their tracks, which I soon lost. I had possessed the philosophers' stone for one lightning flash. Can one find it a second time, when even the first time all search is in vain? Chance was my only hope. I did not meet those two; nor even two others like them. In fact it seemed that the streets were being deserted, and when the ringing of a horsedrawn tram had subsided in the distance, I was left to my own devices in a stony moonlit landscape, veiled in the snow that drifted icily from outer space against the dockside warehouses. Only special landmarks gave me a clue to my whereabouts. The angel who keeps his torch lowered over the names of the fallen emerged from the gloom. For a moment it seemed comforting to me that my brother's name was among those on the memorial tablet, and that probably, therefore, he was one of those who knew the word and had no need to run about in the snow to look for it. There was the low wall that usually gave one a view of the port. That day there was something unusual about it. Had someone put down his baggage, a half-filled kitbag, and left it there for the snow to settle on? Or had they set up a piece of sculpture there to flatter the townspeople's artistic sense in sun and snow? I went closer and saw a man crouching on the para-

pet half covered with snow like an abandoned kitbag
or like a stone figure that endures every kind of
weather.

In the open air.

PAUL. A fine hour to sit about with no roof over your
  head.

LAPARTE. Who would find me if I stayed at home?

PAUL. Did you want to be found? Well, I've found
  you. Even though I was looking for something
  different.

LAPARTE. Tonight there's nothing better to be sought
  or found than me.

PAUL. That sounds promising.

LAPARTE. Would you like to touch my hump?

PAUL. What for?

LAPARTE. They say it's lucky. Remember, this is the
  first night of the year. Luckier than a horseshoe, a
  four-leaved clover, or a chimney-sweep. Enough
  luck for the whole year, and you can have it for a
  silver dollar.

PAUL. More than I can afford.

LAPARTE. Half a dollar then, as it's nearly morning.

PAUL. I should feel I was getting it too cheap. Is
  there no fixed price?

LAPARTE. You are ignorant, but –

PAUL. Well?

LAPARTE. But have it in you to become one of those
  who know. Here's my hump.

PAUL. You're frozen.

LAPARTE. That doesn't astonish me.

PAUL. Come back with me and warm yourself. I'll make some tea.

LAPARTE. But what if another should come, in need of luck?

PAUL. Drunks are happy, and the night is over. No one will come now. Does it work when the night is over?

LAPARTE. Not so well.

PAUL. Come on, then.

Paul's studio.

PAUL. Punch would have warmed you even better But I thought that maybe you'd had enough of New Year's night.

LAPARTE. What about you?

PAUL. I drank till two o'clock in the morning. Grog punch and wine.

LAPARTE. Are you a painter?

PAUL. As you see.

LAPARTE. Very true to life.

PAUL. Feeling warmer already?

LAPARTE. The jackdaw there, the lapwing. And what about that one over there, the unfinished one? Can't make much of it yet.

PAUL. A fox coming out of the wood. I often paint it, always the same way. A popular prize for rifle club competitions.

LAPARTE: Very neat piece of work, I must say. So that gecko over there.

PAUL. You're quite an expert. Will you have a biscuit?

LAPARTE. Thanks.

PAUL. Early on New Year's Day biscuits are best.

LAPARTE. Do you paint other things too, portraits, historical scenes?

PAUL. No.

LAPARTE. Only animals?

PAUL. Only animals.

LAPARTE. Excellent.

PAUL. Why should it be excellent?

LAPARTE. It seemed so to me.

PAUL. Let me fill your cup.

LAPARTE. I feel much warmer now. I shall be going soon.

PAUL. Did I seem churlish? I find my paintings abominable.

LAPARTE. I don't know anything about paintings, but I do know about animals. That's why I said they were good.

PAUL. And it could be that I was churlish because it wasn't you I was looking for.

LAPARTE. Who then?

PAUL. Let's say a man with a silk hat and a lady with a jaunty toque.

LAPARTE. A pity it's me, so that it may seem presumptuous of me to say ...

PAUL. Go on, say it.

LAPARTE. What a man finds is what he's been looking for.

PAUL. What I was looking for was a word.

LAPARTE. A word?

PAUL. A particular word.

LAPARTE. Out in the street?

PAUL. Why not? Wait a minute. I'm close to it now.

There must have been an A very near the beginning – at least I think so. But it's easy to be mistaken.

LAPARTE. A word you've heard?

PAUL. Not *a* word, the word. The only word.

LAPARTE. In that case there's no A in it.

PAUL. I think there is. It could have been Greek or Latin.

LAPARTE. Really?

PAUL. It sounded like – yes, like 'Lacertis'.

LAPARTE. Lacertis?

PAUL. No, that's not it.

   (LAPARTE *laughs*.)

   But it could have been something like it.

LAPARTE. Something like!

PAUL. That's the nearest I can get. Lacertis! Yes, it was almost that.

LAPARTE. Almost!

PAUL. Lacertis ...

LAPARTE. You've missed your chance. You won't find it now.

PAUL. You talk as though you knew.

LAPARTE. I know a great many words, just as far away from the real one as –

PAUL. Lacertis?

LAPARTE. Once uttered they fall on the ground like stones. Lacertis –

PAUL. Pretty meaningless, eh?

LAPARTE. It suggests lizards – Latin, *lacertus* – and must have something to do with reptiles.

PAUL (*meditatively*). Lizards.

   (LAPARTE *laughs*.)

   Why do you laugh?

LAPARTE. I've written a book on lizards.

PAUL (*after a brief hesitation*). That sounds implausible.

LAPARTE. A fad of mine.

PAUL. And I pick you up in the street after hearing that very word?

LAPARTE. That very word is what you didn't hear.

PAUL (*confused*). So many coincidences.

LAPARTE. Too many, almost. The lizard, by the way, is connected with clairvoyance too. Consider Apollo –

PAUL. That, in turn, reminds me of last night. Would you call this a lizard by any chance?

LAPARTE (*mockingly*). What, cast in lead?

PAUL. Manuela thought it was an archway.

LAPARTE. Manuela is probably right. Much more like an archway than a lizard.

PAUL. A pity; it would have fitted in so well. (*He laughs – they both laugh.*)

LAPARTE. Do you feel like coming to Brazil with me?

PAUL. A New Year joke?

LAPARTE. A scientific expedition. I could use someone who can paint lizards.

PAUL (*laughs*). As accurately as I do?

LAPARTE. Half the expenses would be borne by the Belgian Academy of Science, the other half by me.

PAUL. By you? Out of the profit you made on New Year's Eve?

LAPARTE. Year after year I've wondered why everyone chose to invite me on New Year's Eve, when no one gives me a thought all the rest of the year – the way I've lived in Antwerp I might just as well have been in the Sahara or among the seals.

PAUL. It's Antwerp, then.

E

LAPARTE. Then I saw that it was my hump that made me so attractive. Ever since then I've left my home town at the New Year. I go to Paris or Amsterdam, London, Cologne or Hamburg. My hump is always welcome.

PAUL. For a silver dollar?

LAPARTE. One has to ask for money. Luck doesn't count if you get it for nothing.

PAUL. You didn't make *me* pay.

LAPARTE. Because you won't have any luck.

PAUL. You're very blunt.

LAPARTE. Come along to Brazil, then. You won't miss anything here.

PAUL. And over there?

LAPARTE. That lump of lead was wrongly interpreted. Not an archway but a ship. The one that goes to Pernambuco. A good omen.

PAUL. Didn't you say that I shan't have any luck?

LAPARTE. Think it over. I'll drop you a line. And I should be inclined to say: in many ways luck consists in having none.

PAUL (*narrating*). I took my strange guest to the station, where, in patched shoes, threadbare over-coat and hatless, he got on the train to Brussels and stretched out for the night on the red plush of a first-class carriage. Maybe he really was from Antwerp, maybe he really owned ocean-going ships? Nothing was impossible. As I walked home it occurred to me that I didn't even know his name. Did he know mine? Well, it didn't matter much; the thought of Brazil didn't fill me with irresistible longing. Back in my room the piece of lead still lay on the table. Was it a ship? I granted myself that 'archway' was the more convincing version. Then the thought struck me that only one night had passed since the lead had dropped with a hiss into cold water. Also, that on Manuela's account I might be reluctant to leave the town, and I recalled that she too had spoken of lizards, though in her story they'd had no real significance.

Algeciras atmosphere.

MANUELA (*narrating: contrasting acoustic*). Our house was up on the hillside above the town and you could look across the bay to the rock of Gibraltar. A white, dazzling road led up to our house from the harbour. My favourite hiding-place was the hedge on our side of the low garden wall. There you had the best view of everything, and could see people right down below, very tiny, with very tiny carts and very tiny donkeys and very tiny boats, with red sails. Even the great ships in the harbour were tiny, and the still larger ones out at sea were even tinier. All this was so far away that often I was afraid we should be forgotten in our cool, white, tall house. At times someone came up the road, and that was a comfort. I was thirteen or fourteen, and had a great craving for people. But I only dared to be close to them when I lay behind my hedge. Otherwise I'd run away from them like a kid which a stranger tries to lure away from the nanny-goat. And yet I knew everyone likely to come that way: old Victoria, who delivered our meat and vegetables, the postman, the four labourers who worked in the half-disused quarry where the road came to an end. I still know the names of those four: Ramón, José, Ricardo, Carlos, and at night, when they came back from the quarry, Ramón, Ricardo, Carlos, José. At night the order was always a bit different from what it was in the morning. Only once did a stranger come along. He came along at the hottest hour of the afternoon, and I saw him a long way off, appearing and vanishing again according to the bends in the road. He wore a peaked cap which he pushed back from time to time to wipe his forehead, and when he came closer I saw that he must be a sailor from one of the two boats that had docked last night in our harbour. Why was he coming up this way? It was a long and hot climb that led nowhere but to our house and the quarry. By now I could have seen his face, but he kept his head lowered as he slowly mounted. He stopped near the wall and looked up to the hedge, and looked at the very place where I lay hidden. Though I was sure that he couldn't see me, I felt that I was being seen. But I remained there, crouching just as motionless as the lizard that was basking there on top of the wall. For a few moments I saw the man clearly. He was obviously very young, with a fair but tanned complexion, thin lips and blue, very bright eyes. With those bright blue eyes he stared fixedly at my hiding-place, and it seemed as though he didn't blink once all that time. When he'd first raised his head, I hadn't known him, but after those few seconds he was familiar to me, I'd known him for a long time, he was like a brother with whom I'd grown up and I loved him. Suddenly he swung round and went back the way he had come. My heart contracted, but it was natural that he should go. He went down the road, disappeared behind trees and rocks, emerged again and became smaller and smaller till he was one of those tiny creatures that swarmed about the harbour alleys, and till I no longer knew which of those creatures was he. He had come up all that way to look at the hedge behind which I was hiding; he had come to make himself known. That had been done, and there was no reason for him to stay longer.

PAUL (*narrating*). While I was recollecting the previous evening and Manuela in this way, I fell asleep at the table. Visible from far away and for a long time, a dazzling white sail cut into my sleep and it was also the resolve to look up Manuela. When I awoke, however, this resolve seemed questionable to me. I made some tea and went back to my work on a picture which should really have been delivered by Christmas time. Perhaps it was better to run into Manuela again casually. In the course of the next few days I finished the painting and started on a new one exactly like it for an art dealer at Ingolstadt. Having no real pretext for a visit, I decided that a letter was indicated. I finished the second painting, and a third. Outside, it snowed. I rarely left the house. Then I received a letter from a Mr Laparte in Antwerp. I was to come soon and make all the necessary arrangements. I quickly painted the last three orders for 'Fox breaking covert', sold my furniture, and one morning went to the station with a medium-sized suitcase. I had the impression that it had never stopped snowing in the meantime. I spent

three weeks at Laparte's house, where he lived alone
with a large staff of servants. Then the ship sailed
for Pernambuco.

*Docks. Ship's siren and sound of engines up and
under.*

PAUL (*narrating*). The ship to Pernambuco. I can't
have got to Brazil any other way. But I search my
memory for a ship and a long sea voyage. My
memory has dismissed a great deal – things, I
assume, for which it has no further use. But there's
no one now whom I might ask how long the crossing took and at what ports we called. I can see us
all at Dr Bayard's house. I see his round grey beard
and his dark eyes behind the pince-nez. He comes
from Normandy and Laparte values him as an auth-
ority on snakes. He is the society doctor of Pernambuco. His sister keeps house for him, a shy old maid.
I think she's either dumb or a phantom. There are
times when her quietness is frightening.

The ship to Pernambuco. It has been broken up
and its name forgotten in obsolete registers. There it
is again, that suspicious word: forgotten. It insinu-
ates itself everywhere. I shouldn't like to think that
it is the little coin which I carried under my tongue
and had to give the ferryman for my passage. After
all, we were very gay at Dr Bayard's house, drank
Brazilian red wine and real burgundy, and smoked
black cigars. We must have spent a few weeks there.
I learnt a bit of Portuguese, bought provisions, hired
mulattoes, and did oil paintings of the snakes which

Dr Bayard kept in glass cases. Laparte was the busiest of us all and made careful preparations for everything. The Indios were afraid of his deformity, and this gave him power over them. But I forgot to say that there were four of us. There was also Zeemans, and Kingsley. All wanted to collect something or other. Zeemans, beetles and flies, Kingsley, spearheads, cups and feather ornaments. It may be, too, that Kingsley collected beetles and Zeemans spearheads; I've forgotten, as I've forgotten the ship to Pernambuco. Sometimes I wonder whether it wasn't called Lacertis, since for some time the most unlikely thing has seemed the most plausible to me. For me that name would have a certain irony. For evidently the purpose of this lizard expedition was to show me that the word Lacertis could mean a great number of things as soon as one supposed that it meant anything at all. As for what Dr Bayard said to me, at first I didn't take it very seriously. But my conversation with him has remained clear in my memory, more than anything else that we may have discussed at Pernambuco before leaving for the interior.

Room. Outside, Brazilian street atmosphere.

BAYARD. Mr Laparte wants to stay eighteen months?
PAUL. Roughly that.
BAYARD. And you can stay as long as you please?
PAUL. Yes.
BAYARD. What will you do when Mr Laparte has gone?

PAUL. I always do the same thing: I paint.

BAYARD. Do you think that you can live by painting in Brazil?

PAUL. In Brazil? I want to live in Europe.

BAYARD. Mr Laparte told me that you wouldn't be going back to Europe.

PAUL. You must have misunderstood him.

BAYARD. He told me that you've given up your flat and that there's nothing to keep you in Europe.

PAUL. Nor is there anything to keep me in Brazil.

BAYARD. I too arrived one day, with nothing to keep me here. That was forty years ago, and I've been here ever since.

PAUL. But why should I spend my life here?

BAYARD. I don't know you. Mr Laparte knows you better.

PAUL. I first met him three months ago.

BAYARD. And yet you've joined his expedition?

PAUL. Only because it happened that way. And really it all hinged on one word. Mr Laparte took it for a kind of portent, if you can use such big words about our acquaintance.

BAYARD. A word, you say. What word?

PAUL. It was Lacertis, and it reminded him of his lizards.

BAYARD. Lacertis?

PAUL. I overheard it one night.

BAYARD. Where?

PAUL. Through the open window. A couple of drunks. I guessed that it was of some significance for me.

BAYARD (absent-mindedly). Of some significance for you.

PAUL. No doubt a groundless supposition. And it may not be the word I overheard.

BAYARD. It could have a different meaning.

PAUL. That's what Mr Laparte thinks too.

BAYARD. Lacertis. And just a shade different.

PAUL. There'd be quite a few shades to choose from.

BAYARD. I have grounds enough for distinguishing my shade from the others.

PAUL. Yours? What are its implications?

BAYARD. Laertes – that was your word.

PAUL. Would that make better sense?

BAYARD. The father of Odysseus.

PAUL. Those wanderings, Ithaca?

BAYARD. The wanderings *and* Ithaca.

PAUL. Significant for me, you'd say?

BAYARD. For me.

PAUL. For you?

BAYARD. Because I have a son.

PAUL (*laughs*). Odysseus?

BAYARD. That's what I've called him at times in my own mind. But till now it wasn't clear to me that this would make me Laertes.

PAUL. It may be so. Perhaps my word *was* Laertes. It could have been Laertes, and could have been something quite different.

BAYARD. Laertes. That's the name which fits me.

PAUL. And you mean I heard it only for your sake? Only to bring it to you? Only to tell it to you as we stand here looking down at that empty, sun-drenched square?

BAYARD. Yes. Only for that.

PAUL (*laughs*). And I suppose that now at last I know why I came to Pernambuco?

BAYARD. As we all know, Odysseus returned.

PAUL. None of us ever learnt a different version. If you want to trust Homer –

BAYARD. Homer and the drunken man in the night. To me too Odysseus will return, though he has travelled the seas for twelve years.

PAUL (*narrating*). We went up the Amazon in the paddle steamer and established our permanent quarters some hundreds of miles beyond Manaos. I was kept busy painting everything that Laparte caught; for he was afraid that few of the creatures would survive the voyage back to Europe, and wanted to bring them back as pictures at least. For Zeemans and Kingsley, too, I did some paintings. Happy days, when I sat in the shade in front of the hut, mixing colours. Naked, chattering Indian children surrounded me, and again and again they longed to taste those dabs of colour, just as our children long for coloured sweets. It was hard to keep the tubes safe from them, for there might have been poisonous paints among them. Sometimes too there was no one standing about my easel, and then I heard their cries down by the river, where they were bathing, and perhaps there would be an ancient, pipe-smoking Indian woman, very ugly and as dirty as she was ugly, come to see my painting. Around dusk the smell of fish or game drifted out of the huts and the smell of maize bread and strong spices. Then the others came home from their fieldwork, we ate the meals which our native cook had prepared for us, and they commented on my paintings. They were severely critical if some mark on a reptile's back was not yellow enough or a red wasn't quite the natural shade. Before going to sleep they often complained of the moist heat. It didn't worry me at all, and in those sultry nights I slept under my mosquito net as though I'd never known anything different. Happy days – I don't know whether they amounted to weeks or months. One evening, as we sat eating, they ended; without my noticing, Laparte's words put an end to them.

Half-open room. Outside, atmosphere of native village in jungle.

LAPARTE. I got them to paddle me to a new place today. I had the feeling that this locality is exhausted for my purposes. What about you?

ZEEMANS. It's all the same to me. I can find the things anywhere – as many as I need.

KINGSLEY. A change would be better for me.

LAPARTE. By the way, I hear that there's a white man three days' journey from here, with another tribe.

ZEEMANS. Who'd be useful to us?

LAPARTE. Who is lying ill there.

PAUL. Since when?

LAPARTE. I couldn't discover the precise circumstances.

ZEEMANS. Malaria, I suppose.

LAPARTE. I don't know. It was all a bit vague.

KINGSLEY (*yawns*). Someone ought to look into it some time.

PAUL. I wonder why the Indians don't move him on.

KINGSLEY. Or why they haven't done him in, you might also wonder.

ZEEMANS. Yes, there are all sorts of questions one could ask.

PAUL. It would be best to ask him.

LAPARTE. That's what I thought. One of us should go there. Drugs, some tea, a blanket –

ZEEMANS. Very thoughtful of you.

KINGSLEY. That reduces all the questions to one.

LAPARTE. Who's going?

ZEEMANS. I'm rather behind with the cataloguing.

KINGSLEY. There's no need for me to explain why I can't get away at this moment.

PAUL. You seem to be looking at me, Mr Laparte.

LAPARTE. Only because I'm waiting to hear your reason for not going.

ZEEMANS. But perhaps it would matter least to you ...

KINGSLEY. Whether you do your painting here or take a little trip up the river.

ZEEMANS. Bound to find some good subjects on the way.

KINGSLEY. Yes, and a change of company at last.

Up atmosphere of river journey, and fade under.

PAUL (*narrating*). The hut in which Richards lay ill was in bad condition. It was evening, and through the chinks in the wall light penetrated and formed a barrier between him and me. He lay in one corner on a bed of dry leaves. A bowl and a jug were beside him, and that was all. As I entered he propped himself up and turned his face towards me; or rather turned what had once been his face.

Distant atmosphere of native village in the hut.

RICHARDS. Please get out.

PAUL. We heard about you and thought we might be able to help in some way.

RICHARDS. There's nothing I need.

PAUL. Is it malaria?

RICHARDS. It's leprosy. That's why I advise you to leave.

PAUL. Oh, it can't be all that infectious.

RICHARDS. One could even say, not infectious at all.

PAUL. Why should I go, then?

RICHARDS. I don't much like being looked at.

PAUL. There are things one could do for you. You're not lying comfortably.

RICHARDS. Insecticide, disinfectant, bars on the window, barbed wire about the place. I've heard enough about all those things. I want to die the way it suits me.

PAUL. You won't be doing that just yet.

RICHARDS. I've paid for it with filth and vermin; it's a simple account.

PAUL. Who brings you food and drink?

RICHARDS. The Indians. They help me out of fear.

PAUL. I'm afraid too, I could help you too.

RICHARDS. Go, I tell you; the others went.

PAUL. What others?

RICHARDS. I've thought of something I could do with.

PAUL. What is it? Maybe –

RICHARDS. Whisky.

PAUL. Do you think it would be good for you?

RICHARDS. That isn't the point.

PAUL. Who were the others?

RICHARDS. Nor is that – now. Have you brought any whisky?

PAUL. There's some back at our camp. A few days' journey from here.

RICHARDS. Will you fetch it?

PAUL. Yes.

RICHARDS. There were four of us. When they realized what it was, they cleared out. I've been here a year. (*With animation*) Really whisky wouldn't be at all a bad thing. But I don't believe you'll come back.

PAUL. Wait and see.

RICHARDS. Besides, I'd rather you didn't come back than have you treat me as a sort of poor Lazarus.

PAUL. Did you say Lazarus?

RICHARDS. There's a kind of pity, you know –

PAUL. What made you think of Lazarus?

RICHARDS. How could I fail to think of him?

PAUL. It reminds you of Lacertis, doesn't it?

RICHARDS. Of what?

PAUL. Perhaps it won't be me, after all, who brings you the whisky. There are four of us. I shall have to consult the others.

RICHARDS. The others – they're the ones a man should distrust.

PAUL. I should be happier if Lacertis were connected only with lizards.

RICHARDS. When I look at you, I can well imagine your staying here in my place, even without having leprosy. (*He laughs.*)

PAUL. Aren't you presuming rather?

RICHARDS. It's the small presumption of those who take a long time to die. Of course, it's no less irritating for that. But please don't think that I'm complaining. It's a pleasant disease which doesn't hurt. One grows insensitive. What more can one ask?

PAUL (*narrating*). I was full of resentment against Richards, much as I pitied him. To be left to rot alive, abandoned by everyone, was that a good reason for being presumptuous? Were people fools just because they weren't sick? Let the others get his whisky! I'd gone on the first trip. The second wasn't my business.

River journey atmosphere fades into open air, Indian background.

PAUL. Not infectious, he says.

ZEEMANS. I hope you took the necessary precautions all the same.

LAPARTE. Some Lysol in the water when you wash.

ZEEMANS. That's not enough.

PAUL. Look, if you're worried –

LAPARTE. Don't let us quarrel now, please.

KINGSLEY. Infectious or not, there's precious little we can do for the fellow.

ZEEMANS. Poor devil.

KINGSLEY. Where are you off to?

ZEEMANS. I'm turning in. Had a hard day.

LAPARTE. I wish you a good night, Zeemans.

PAUL. Have we had easy days?

KINGSLEY. No. Or yes. In any case, let's try to make the next ones easier.

PAUL. That's no problem. Apart from Richards.

LAPARTE. So it's whisky he wants.

KINGSLEY. Have we got enough?

PAUL. He's ill.

KINGSLEY. And whisky will do him more harm than good.

LAPARTE. I'm not so sure.

PAUL. I'm quite sure that it will make no difference to his state of health.

KINGSLEY (*decisively*). I propose that we take him to the coast. There's sure to be an institution somewhere for such cases. That's where he belongs.

LAPARTE. This possibility has one advantage: it would look as though we'd done something for the man.

KINGSLEY. Well?

LAPARTE. And at the same time it might look as though we'd done nothing for him.

KINGSLEY. Getting him there – is that nothing?

LAPARTE. All right then, let's take him to the coast.

PAUL. And pack up the expedition?

LAPARTE. How so?

PAUL. Didn't you say we'd take him down to the coast?

LAPARTE. One of us will do.

PAUL (*narrating*). The following morning Zeemans and Kingsley set out so early that I never saw them again. I packed what I needed for my second journey to Richards. Laparte joined me and watched me with his quick little eyes. I hated him at that moment.

In front of the hut.

LAPARTE. A pity you're leaving us. So many days when you won't be painting, so many pictures the less for me.

PAUL. I ought to take my sea boots.

LAPARTE. If you consider the matter a little longer you'll discover that there's nothing you should not take.

PAUL. You're right. I'm packing too many things.

LAPARTE. On the contrary – too few. Are you going to leave your painting tackle?

PAUL. Do you think I'm going to have any time for painting?

LAPARTE. It will take you a week to get to Manaos, and three weeks to Para.

PAUL. How will he survive it? It's more like a journey from one graveyard to another.

LAPARTE. That's true of every journey – more or less.

PAUL. Or at best to a kind of prison.

LAPARTE. But among his own kind.

PAUL. Now don't talk about 'shared suffering'.

LAPARTE. I was just about to. Or should we not take him to the coast?

PAUL. I'm always the one who has to decide when both alternatives are equally bad. You people just turn round and go on collecting lizards or beetles.

LAPARTE. And you're the one to whom we leave human beings. In the Middle Ages, incidentally, lepers carried rattles which they had to use when they approached inhabited places. People threw them bread or money.

PAUL. I'm afraid of your learned digressions.

LAPARTE. They called them Lazarus rattles.

PAUL. Now don't try to tell me that Richards concerns me alone. I will take him some whisky, no more.

LAPARTE. No one is reproaching you.

PAUL. I shall take enough luggage for a few days.

LAPARTE. We shall be moving our headquarters within the next few days. It would be better for you to have all your things when you're looking for us.

PAUL. *All* my things?

LAPARTE. That's my advice.

PAUL. And what if I left some of them here?

LAPARTE. There would be a risk of theft.

PAUL. Or what if you took them?

LAPARTE. It always turns out that one's packed the wrong things.

PAUL. An answer to every question. But no more.

LAPARTE. And you'll bear in mind that money has been deposited in your name at Manaos, Para and Pernambuco. Don't forget.

Up river journey atmosphere and under.

PAUL (narrating). Lazarus. For days, while I was being paddled upstream the word obsessed me; I *thought* the word. I thought it with its three vowels and four consonants, and now I know that you can think a word. It moves, moves very fast and always straight ahead, an arrow shot from a bow – notched to the string it was once at rest, precariously, but still at rest. The marksman is unknown; and no one can be sure where the target is, or whether the arrow was shot senselessly into void and chance. To the right and to the left, above and below, images light up briefly, as in a lightning flash. They are too clear to last. Lazarus, biblical garments, a stern hand that bars all accidents.

The sores, all the sores in the world, garish pictures out of medical textbooks, and we know what a horror the body is. What if we could see the soul in colour? The houses, agglomerations of houses, homesteads despairingly scattered over the landscape, horses, cows, flocks of sheep, all exerting themselves, but without avail. Libraries full of books, each a wordy concealment of loneliness. Roads which lead nowhere but back to our starting point. Prospects that please – as if we had any prospects.

Lazarus. Are there words that do not contain the world? A man lying in a hut in the jungle with leprosy. He waits for death. He is no worse off than anyone else. He is well enough. No need to bother with him. A few bottles of whisky, and off you go. A waste of good whisky. The idea that one should be concerned about everyone, that's sentimentality. And the escape from it? Professional concern : midwives, nurses, doctors, priests, gravediggers, keeners, paid welfare workers of every kind – you should leave it to them.

And meanwhile, the suspicion, no, by now the certainty, that Richards was blind. Did he still have any eyes at all?

River and jungle atmosphere up.

PAUL. Could I endure the sight of that face, which was no longer a face, for more than an hour? Screams, shrieks from the bank. From the monkeys in the trees, or maybe parrots. Soon I shall wake up. But where shall I be lying then?

Lazarus, Lazarus.

River out, jungle background remains, up Indian village. Hut acoustic.

PAUL. No soda, you'll have to drink it neat. You'll feel as thirsty as the damned in Hell.

RICHARDS. I'm used to Hell.

PAUL. We think it our duty to take you to the coast.

RICHARDS. The devil take you as well!

PAUL. I can't force you.

RICHARDS. Whisky tasted better in my memory. But I shall get used to the taste again.

PAUL. There's hardly enough of it for you to get used to it again.

RICHARDS. You in a hurry to get away?

PAUL. No hurry, but –

RICHARDS. Put the bottle closer. How many have you got?

PAUL. Three.

RICHARDS. Three days, you might call it.

PAUL. A little more, perhaps.

RICHARDS. And what about you? Three days, three hours, or? (*When Paul does not reply*) Frightened? But it isn't easy to catch the thing. Catching leprosy is almost as hard as finding happiness. (*He laughs.*) You need to have a talent for it. Just think how few lepers there are.

PAUL. How did you catch it?

RICHARDS. I've been in too many ports and slept in too many beds to know for sure. It started five years ago. A few patches of red on the skin, on one thigh and on the belly, that was all. It went, and came back in different places. I paid no attention to it. But you don't want to listen to a case history. And really I know quite well how I caught it. I mean, what it was in me that made me catch it, that enabled me to catch it, if you like.

PAUL. A predisposition, you suggested.

RICHARDS. I mean that point in the world where all things are decided.

PAUL. Is there such a point?

RICHARDS. I was on a Turkish ship at the time, and we'd called at Algeciras. There's no port quite so dead. And of course it isn't really a port, but a fishing village. Red wine is the only amenity. I complained about this to the landlord at the *fonda*, and he laughed and said Algeciras was the centre of the world, because everything stands still there and everything else revolves about it.

PAUL. Where's the centre of the world, did you say?

RICHARDS. At Algeciras. I don't think you're listening.

PAUL. Go on all the same.

RICHARDS. I went back on board, but next day for some reason we couldn't sail, and were bored again. By noon I couldn't stand any more of the local amusements. I strolled round the streets, and came to a road that wound up the hill. Walking up that hill in the heat wasn't exactly a pleasure; I wasn't going anywhere, but boredom drove me on. Suddenly I was at the centre of the world.

PAUL. At Algeciras.

RICHARDS. To be more precise, some way above Algeciras. The road made a bend there, there was a high wall and a hedge above it. A lizard sat on top of the wall, with its head raised, as though petrified half-way through some movement. But I had the feeling that a pair of eyes was gazing at me through the hedge, eyes which I couldn't see.

PAUL. Yes.

RICHARDS. Algeciras is near Gibraltar. You can look across to the rock.

PAUL. The road led up to a quarry.

RICHARDS. A quarry? Could be.

PAUL. But you didn't walk on.

RICHARDS. I didn't walk on. Have I told you the story before?

PAUL. No.

RICHARDS. I often tell it. To the tree-trunks and the water-jug.

PAUL. And after that!

RICHARDS (confused). After that?

PAUL. A pair of eyes looked at you.

RICHARDS. Or the hedge itself.

PAUL. But you didn't hear anything? No sound, no word?

RICHARDS. Only the silence of Algeciras, around which the world revolved.

PAUL. And then?

RICHARDS. Then? No then. There was no then for me

at that moment. And I couldn't stand it either. I turned on my heel and left, so that the lizard might run on and the eyes in the hedge might be those of a girl staring inquisitively at me as I went. In order that it might be so, I turned on my heel and left. Do you follow me? So that everything might be forgotten.

PAUL. I understand. But was everything forgotten?

RICHARDS. Algeciras was as before: the *fonda*, the port, the ship. And yet I tried in vain to see it as I'd seen it only an hour before. (*With more animation*) A familiar experience: you see a town for the first time. But then you live there for a long time, your view of it changes more and more, and you never see it again as you saw it in that first moment.

PAUL. Never again?

RICHARDS. Perhaps at times, as in a flash.

PAUL. But a flash of joy.

RICHARDS. When I walked down the hill I had spent many years in Algeciras. But there was something else. I never again saw anything anywhere as in that first moment. I knew everything, I had lived everywhere for a long time. And that's what leprosy really is. I caught it because I already had it.

PAUL. Is your sight still good?

RICHARDS. It's gradually going now. The worse I see, the newer everything becomes for me. I live backwards. Death – that's the moment when the world is as on the first day.

PAUL (*narrating*). The Indians who looked after Richards cleared a hut for me to live in during my stay. Richards was never fully awake for more than

87

a few hours each day, spending the rest in a kind of coma. I had the feeling that he wasn't very far from that moment of which he'd spoken. The idea of taking him down to the coast became more and more absurd. I had a good deal of time on my hands, and unpacked my painting gear. I didn't paint animals this time, I painted the hut in which Richards was to die, the path that led to it, and the jungle behind it. I thought I was painting this for Manuela. There was no need to tell her that death was part of the picture. It was a jungle landscape, nothing more. It was the best I ever painted, but bad enough all the same. Manuela never saw the picture. I suppose there are many things which concern me but which I never learn about, just as Manuela was never to know that painting. The whisky lasted longer than expected but on the sixth day it was finished. I considered the possibility of which no one had spoken; indeed, it seemed to me the most natural.

In the hut.

RICHARDS. You don't offer me anything today.

PAUL. The bottles are empty.

RICHARDS. And three days have passed?

PAUL. This is the sixth.

RICHARDS. You've stayed longer than you intended. Weren't you going to take me to the coast?

PAUL. You didn't want me to.

RICHARDS. You'll have to be going now, won't you?

PAUL. I'm staying.

RICHARDS. How long?

PAUL. I don't know.

RICHARDS. I know.

PAUL. I thought I'd stay as long as you want.

RICHARDS. When the time comes I shan't be wanting anything. You'll be bored. Would you light the candle, please?

PAUL. The candle?

RICHARDS. That's what I said.

PAUL. I've run out of candles.

RICHARDS. And now I see that it's broad daylight. The sun is shining on my hand. It's nearly time now, or I shall know darkness too long.

PAUL (*narrating*). On the tenth day a canoe arrived, to my surprise. The Indians drew me to the bank with their cries. There was Laparte, smaller and more hunchbacked than ever. In his white shirt he looked like a kitbag covered with snow, dumped indifferently and abandoned – just as he'd looked when I first set eyes on him. A harbour wall in winter, or the sun on the Amazon – the differences were slighter than one might suppose, great at first, but cancelling themselves out in time.

In the open air. Village and jungle.

LAPARTE. I had the feeling that this was your 'at home' day, Paul.

PAUL. All my days have been so, recently. Anything in particular?

LAPARTE. Only my need for company and conversation.

PAUL. That house in front of us is mine.

LAPARTE. And Richards?

PAUL. Next door.

LAPARTE. He still – lives in it?

PAUL. Yes.

LAPARTE. Not a bad place.

PAUL. Not bad for what?

LAPARTE. To live in, of course.

PAUL. This way in. Take the folding chair.

LAPARTE. Ah, so you're painting again? New subjects?

PAUL. Only to occupy myself.

LAPARTE. You're short of lizards.

PAUL. If you say so.

LAPARTE. It's of your hut, isn't it? A souvenir.

PAUL. Richards' hut.

LAPARTE. A souvenir all the same.

PAUL. I suppose so.

LAPARTE. I'm surprised to find you still here. Shouldn't you have been on your way to the coast long ago? Wasn't that your plan?

PAUL. I'm staying a bit longer. That's to say, he's staying a bit longer.

LAPARTE. It comes to the same thing.

PAUL. The difference wouldn't be worth a quarrel.

LAPARTE. I haven't come here to quarrel. I wanted to ask you whether you'd come with me.

PAUL. No.

LAPARTE. Of course not. You'd already answered that question.

PAUL. Everything all right at base camp?

LAPARTE. Everything all right. I'm on my own there now.

PAUL. How so? Zeemans and Kingsley?

LAPARTE. If you recall, the northern tributary widens into a kind of lake after an hour's journey.

PAUL. You mean, the others have gone off by themselves?

LAPARTE. That route didn't suit me.

PAUL. But only a short time before you yourself had proposed –

LAPARTE. Second thoughts.

PAUL. A quarrel?

LAPARTE. Not a quarrel. Only Kingsley and Zeemans are annoyed, and rightly so.

PAUL. Why rightly?

LAPARTE. My decision to terminate the expedition as far as I was concerned took them rather by surprise.

PAUL. Me too.

LAPARTE. Irresponsibility is what Kingsley called it.

PAUL. And what are your plans now?

LAPARTE. My plans! (*He laughs.*) Yes, it's difficult to explain, I have no excuse to offer really. Except my hump. And no one will suffer financially.

PAUL. No one will attribute it to meanness.

LAPARTE. It may be the heat. Ten years ago it didn't matter to me. Now I can't sleep.

PAUL. That's how thoughts begin.

LAPARTE. And upset my plans. I begin to have doubts, every possible kind of doubt. Why lizards, for instance? Grown-up, serious people travelling for months, to catch lizards. It's absurd. And one turns and turns on one's bed, listening to the mosquitoes. One invents all sorts of reasons for lizards, and all are equally ridiculous. Amongst other

things the thought occurred to me that I collected
lizards only to bring you here.

PAUL. You think too much.

LAPARTE. One morning I get up and it's clear to me
that I never want to see another lizard.

PAUL. And sleep too little.

LAPARTE. It's a fact that most people manage perfectly well without lizards.

PAUL. I'm not so sure.

LAPARTE. That was the day before yesterday.

PAUL. Too short a time for such decisions.

LAPARTE. I shall return to camp from here, pack up,
and be on my way within a few hours. May I repeat my question, whether you would like to
come –

PAUL. Certainly, your question has grown in weight.

LAPARTE. But your answer is the same? (*When Paul
doesn't reply*) You don't need me any more. The
picture, by the way, gets better and better. You've
really brought it off this time. Altogether, it may
be that you'll now find yourself turning to other
subjects.

PAUL (*narrating*). The river flowed broad and muddy.
As the canoe glided into the stream and gathered
speed, Laparte raised one hand and waved to me. He
was standing upright, but it looked as if he'd drawn
his head even lower down between his shoulders and
had sat down exhausted. He called out something to
me, but I didn't catch it. It could have been the
word which I had already once failed to understand.
He had been here, and perhaps he knew it but didn't
tell it to me. But it was possible, too, I thought, that
it could only be told me when the speaker was so far

off that I couldn't catch it. Distance is the pre-requisite of happiness. I raised my hand and waved, although the canoe was no longer recognizable. At the same time I was raising my hand to wipe it all away – all the questions, the many possibilities, the leave-taking, Laparte, Zeemans. Farewell, the river flows broad and muddy, I shall go down that river myself and not return.

In the hut.

RICHARDS. You haven't been to see me all day. Did someone arrive?

PAUL. Yes, and we're in luck; he brought some whisky.

RICHARDS. The lizard man, was it?

PAUL. Two bottles.

RICHARDS. It may be enough.

PAUL. And tinned food.

RICHARDS. Excellent.

PAUL. Will you have a drop?

RICHARDS. Has he left again?

PAUL. He has.

RICHARDS. Where's he going? What will he do? No, that isn't what I want to know. It's something different. What will *you* do when you leave this place?

PAUL. Nothing special, I think.

RICHARDS. One doesn't really know for sure what is special and what isn't. It's special for me, because it will happen at a time when I'm no longer here. You'll be going to Manaos, but will there be such a place as Manaos then? When for me it belongs

93

to the delusions, you'll be walking through those wretched alleys past those cheap bazaars, past the counter of the ship's chandler, Minhos y Filho, and all these things put on a grave face though they no longer exist. Consider that, to the dead, it's the living who are phantoms. And yet you'll go on to Para and Pernambuco. Meanwhile all space will have been suspended, dissolved into something that isn't time either. The boulevards, the cafés, the evening walk, the newspapers, the coins in your purse – all goes on while the music of the spheres has begun to play. (*Laughing*) I'm good at consoling myself, don't you think? (*When Paul doesn't reply*) Then you'll cross the sea. And that, by the way, is something I can envisage even after I am dead. You'll cross the sea. But what will you really be doing?

PAUL. Looking for those eyes that stared at you through the hedge.

RICHARDS. Good God, you can't do the same as I did. Leave that to me – the only occupation that will then remain for me. You have time enough. Here's to a good journey. (*Slight pause.*) Well, won't you wish me the same?

PAUL. Here's to a good journey, Richards.

RICHARDS (*laughing*). That's better.

PAUL (*narrating*). Richards died two weeks later. During most of that time he was unconscious and inarticulate. The Indians helped me to bury him. After taking whatever papers I could find in his kitbag, we burnt the hut and his few possessions. In the evening I read his papers and burnt them also. That night I remained awake for a long time, listening to the night sounds. At times it was loud with animal life, then again one heard only the river, a monotonous roar which certainly would grow imperceptible one day to anyone who remained in this place. I regretted that there was no whisky left, only tobacco for my pipe. This lit up a small space in the hut. Outside there were the stars. I thought of the monument on which my brother's name was inscribed, and thought of Richards, whom I had buried that day, like another brother. When I closed my eyes I saw the first night of that year in my mind, and the falling snow already blotting out the names. The flakes were quick as the night's thoughts. How had I arrived here, at this one point of the world? Had they all, had Manuela, Laparte, Richards, hadn't they all spoken the same word to me? Towards dawn I fell asleep. I dreamed about Manuela.

'Unreal' acoustic. Paul and Manuela different as if they were talking to one another across a distance.

PAUL. Here are the letters, Manuela.

MANUELA. So many of them! A whole coffin full.

PAUL. I've spent my whole life writing them.

MANUELA. When am I to read them all?

PAUL. They all contain the same thing. Only the stamps differ. This one is German, that one Belgian, that one Spanish.

MANUELA. Have you been to Spain?

PAUL. Near Gibraltar.

MANUELA. You haven't been to Spain. And those

letters are not by you. There's nothing written in them. Empty envelopes.

PAUL. My life.

MANUELA. Other people's lives.

PAUL. All that wasn't me, then?

MANUELA. Not even an illness of your own.

PAUL. And I thought –

MANUELA. I thought so too, about myself. But those were different eyes with which I looked through the hedge. I must tell you something, Paul: the path does not lead to the quarry.

PAUL. I thought as much.

MANUELA. But you mustn't tell anyone.

PAUL. I must be off, Manuela. Can't you hear the ship's bells?

MANUELA. They're the bells of all the ships that have run aground.

PAUL. And the captain is a stickler.

MANUELA. Didn't you know, I'm coming with you? I've taken a holiday from work.

PAUL. It's only a small vessel. But if you come with us, there'll be room for all. Come on, then, quick!

PAUL (*narrating*). When I bathed in the river next morning I noticed several red patches on my right hip. Probably it was only that I'd lain in an awkward position during the night, and there was no reason yet to be anxious. By the time I arrived at Manaos – it took me about a week – the patches had gone again, but then suddenly I had them all over my body, and when I took the paddle steamer at Manaos, I could no longer think of any good reasons for not being anxious. It's a slow boat. Often it stops at places for

no purpose that one can see, unless it were to enter-
tain the alligators and parrots. The steamer approaches them with a loud ringing of bells, lies
moored there for an hour or several, with not one
human being to meet it; and then the wheels turn
again and the boat moves on, while the ship's bell
rings meaninglessly into the jungle.

(*Departure of a paddle steamer, ship's bell. Sounds
slowly fade out.*)

In the open air.

PAUL (*narrating*). The bells of all the ships that have
run aground. Laparte said I had no further need of
him : how wrong he was! I need everyone. I need the
groaning old men in the afternoon sun, the infants
in their cradles, the child who can't do his home-
work, the woman knitting by the light of a paraffin
lamp, the doctor who prescribed the wrong medicine,
the drunken man who didn't feel cheerful. Whoever
is afraid, needs them all. I fear for my life, though I
am by no means certain about my illness, Above all,
I need Bayard. He'll tell me whether I've caught it,
and if I have caught it, he'll know of a remedy made
of snakes' venom and orchid juices. It's very comforting, Pernambuco, the sounds of the sea, Dr
Bayard –

Dr Bayard's consulting room. Outside, Brazilian street.

BAYARD. I thought you'd come. I've prepared everything and looked up the relevant literature. (*He titters.*)

PAUL. It appears that the relevant literature is amusing.

BAYARD. It's a rare disease, and one doesn't keep up with rare diseases as a matter of course. I've taken the precaution of examining Laparte also. So I'm in practice already.

PAUL. Laparte? Why, is he still here?

BAYARD. He was till the day before yesterday.

PAUL. I thought as much.

BAYARD. His boat sailed two hours after the funeral.

PAUL. What funeral?

BAYARD. Pretty red, those patches. Any pain?

PAUL. No.

BAYARD. My sister died suddenly.

PAUL. Your sister, did you say?

BAYARD. Oh, you hardly knew her. No point in involving your feelings. As for Laertes – (*Cuts himself short, tensely.*) You see, if I press my finger down here, the impression remains, and the skin doesn't grow taut again.

PAUL. Is that a bad sign?

BAYARD. Nothing is particularly bad.

PAUL. The skin does grow taut again, the impression does not remain.

BAYARD. You know better than I do.

PAUL. If I did, I shouldn't be here.

BAYARD. Just one more puncture, you'll hardly feel it.

PAUL. What were you going to say about Laertes?

BAYARD. That I was mistaken. How long have you had these patches?

PAUL. Five weeks.

BAYARD. I am not that Laertes, Odysseus will not return, this is no Ithaca. This is Pernambuco, a town with a harbour, docks, and a regular mail service. For instance you can receive a letter from Cape Town, and it will take a month at the most. And in it you may well read: Your son has died in the local prison. The date as well, needless to say. And a few official phrases draped around it. But the word 'died' remains legible beneath all the phrases and drapery. How's your appetite? Digestion all right?

PAUL. Doctor Bayard –

BAYARD. You're very sorry, I know. But I asked you –

PAUL. All quite normal.

BAYARD. And why does fate make this vulgar joke? Or rather, you? Why did you make it?

PAUL. I don't follow.

BAYARD. That's done. Your arm again, please. We've nearly finished. Suddenly one day my sister begins to talk madly, and a few days later she's vanished, and on a third day her corpse is found in the harbour pool. For my sake, though, it was described as an accident.

PAUL. Where's the joke, Dr Bayard?

BAYARD. Can't you see it? Can't you see it yet? Laertes. Who induced me to put my trust in that name? Who called me Laertes?

PAUL. You did yourself.

BAYARD. The word came from you. And what we

both forgot, there's another Laertes, not at Ithaca, but at Elsinore. His sister Ophelia, who loved Prince Hamlet, went mad and drowned herself. A fine joke.

PAUL. A joke, you call it?

BAYARD. Laertes! My sister was fifty-nine, and if there was a Prince Hamlet in the case, he must have been bow-legged and bald. Laertes. Just a small confusion over the locality. Very funny, don't you think?

PAUL. Yes.

BAYARD. I must leave you for a moment now. Just a little test in my laboratory, I won't keep you long.

PAUL (*narrating*). I felt as though the jury were retiring for the verdict. Not guilty – attenuating circumstances. I sat on the wooden seat listening for footsteps, the creaking of corridors and the opening and shutting of doors. A long time passed before Dr Bayard returned. But I felt an upsurge of hope when I saw his face. He seemed satisfied.

Consulting room, as before.

PAUL. Well?

BAYARD. As far as your word is concerned, I can provide further variations on it.

PAUL. Touching my state of health?

BAYARD. In my mother tongue there's a word, *la certitude*, certainty.

PAUL. *La certitude.*

BAYARD. Doesn't it make you think of Lacertis? But

what is one sure about, ever? *La certitude*, certainty – it's like an answer to which one doesn't know the question.

PAUL. Is everything all right?

BAYARD. Everything all right.

PAUL. That's all I wanted to know.

(*A ring.*)

BAYARD. Someone to see you, I should think.

PAUL. To see *me*?

BAYARD. Someone who wants to have a word with you.

PAUL. Apart from you, there's no one knows I'm here. Or is there?

BAYARD. Only two gentlemen.

PAUL. Acquaintances of yours?

BAYARD. I've never met them.

(*Another ring.*)

Wait. I'll open the door.

(*He is heard to go out and speak to someone outside.*)

The gentleman will be with you in a moment.

(*He comes back.*)

There are cases of leprosy that develop very fast, I mean develop fatally, a few weeks, or a few months. And there are others that drag themselves out over years, or even decades.

PAUL. That doesn't matter any more.

BAYARD. It continues to matter – always.

PAUL. I mean to me.

BAYARD. And one more thing: the Brazilian home for lepers used to be a monastery, occupied for a very long time by Italian monks. It is still called the Charterhouse, La Certosa.

PAUL. Your ingenuity is boundless, Dr Bayard.

BAYARD. Yes, it does remind you of Lacertis, doesn't it? No one could say that the word is quite meaningless.

PAUL. It certainly does remind me of it – irresistibly.

BAYARD. And you'll have a great deal more leisure to think about it, to acquaint yourself with the re-semblances from the inside, as it were, once you've arrived there.

PAUL. Arrived where?

BAYARD. At the Certosa. The two gentlemen have come to fetch you. Everything is all right, monsieur – you have got leprosy.

PAUL (*narrating*). A two-wheeled cart, on which I lay like a bundle of rags. A mule at the shaft, sore with many beatings, as though it had leprosy too. Stubbornly it pulled us through the wide archway of the Certosa, reluctantly, and I knew that I had arrived. Half the size of a hand and cast in lead – hadn't the pillars and the arch lain on the plush cover of my table? At that time I hadn't known their meaning. To the right and to the left of it the walls were covered with tall shrubs. Through all that growth one could see the pieces of glass at the top, green, brown and white. It was not a hospital that awaited me, but a prison. Whatever the crime, there was no doubt about the sentence. The cells were inhabited by the disintegrating, the blind, by those cripples who crawled on all fours. Their tin plates were outside their doors as I was led through the passage; it was the hour when the beggars' soup was dispensed, and no sick person was allowed to leave his room. Doors were opened secretively behind us, disappointed eyes, disappointed groping hands. But all this didn't become clear to me till later, when I too waited hungry. Not much more than this soup came to us from the outside world, unless one counted Dr Oliveira, our physician, who walked hurriedly through all those passages once a week, and the warders, who kept their distance whenever possible, were really guards, and carried truncheons. As for a priest, there was one among the inmates themselves, and the less serious cases served as gravediggers. Anyone who came to the Certosa was left to his own devices. Soon the rainy season began. It began, and went on, and ended, a new summer began, a new rainy season, three years went by, and suddenly it seemed as though the clocks, which had long come to a stop, started to work once more. This happened when Manuela arrived, the other Manuela. Like me, she arrived when the empty plates were in the passages, and we opened the door and the soup still hadn't been ladled in. A broad mulatto woman in a garish green dress puffed and blew her way through the passage into the deaf-mutes' cell. Manuela was very ill, so obviously ill that it was difficult to understand how she could have remained at liberty until that day. She had lived on garbage and slept under the arches of viaducts. Another beggar had reported her so that she wouldn't have to share her sleeping quarters with Manuela. To Manuela, the Charterhouse was paradise.

THE OTHER MANUELA. The soup isn't as bad as they all say. It's good, very good. There are little bits of meat in it.

PAUL. I like you, Manuela.

THE OTHER MANUELA. Oh Senhor, how can you like me? An old nigger woman with leprosy.

PAUL. I've got leprosy too.

THE OTHER MANUELA. I don't believe it. You're a good-looking man.

PAUL (*laughs*). I like you, Manuela, because your name is Manuela.

THE OTHER MANUELA. Oh, that's a good reason. It's a beautiful name, don't you think?

PAUL. Mightn't all the Manuelas in the world be like one another?

THE OTHER MANUELA. If that's so, Senhor, tell me what the other is like. The one you're thinking of.

PAUL. Am I thinking of one?

THE OTHER MANUELA. I could do my best to be like her.

PAUL. No, you mustn't exert yourself.

THE OTHER MANUELA (*laughs*). Well, confidentially: I am her. I am the other. You only need to forget my colour and my leprosy and a few little things besides. In short: forget me, and I shall be the other.

PAUL. Let's put it to the test, Manuela: where were you born?

THE OTHER MANUELA. I don't know.

PAUL. You're making it too easy for yourself. Do you know Algeciras?

THE OTHER MANUELA. The waiter in the Café Commercial?

PAUL. Algeciras is a town.

THE OTHER MANUELA. Now I remember. The town where I was born. Somewhere near Rio, isn't it?

PAUL. Wrong again, my dear. No, you don't know any of the names, Gibraltar, Antwerp, Laparte, Bayard –

THE OTHER MANUELA. Dr Bayard, do you mean?

PAUL. Do you know him, then?

THE OTHER MANUELA. Once I put my hand in a rubbish bin and a snake bit me.

PAUL. What then?

THE OTHER MANUELA. I went to see him, he hurt me, I don't like to think of Dr Bayard.

PAUL. He got me in here.

THE OTHER MANUELA. I'm not surprised; now he himself is in a house like a prison.

PAUL. What house?

THE OTHER MANUELA. A madhouse.

PAUL. Dr Bayard?

THE OTHER MANUELA. It must be two or three years ago that I went to see him. Soon after that it came out. There was a lot of talk about it in Pernambuco. They put him away when he set his snakes loose.

PAUL. A few years ago?

THE OTHER MANUELA. When I still had my looks; yes, a few years ago.

PAUL (*narrating*). Next day Dr Oliveira paid his visit. After hurriedly going his rounds he retired to the porter's lodge, where he used to spend a few hours writing his reports. I packed my case. There wasn't much to pack, a pair of shoes, three shirts, a pair of trousers, five handkerchiefs, four pairs of socks. That would do for a start. Laparte's money was still waiting for me at the bank. I hoped that a boat would be sailing soon. But even if all went badly I could still be in Europe within five weeks. I wondered how to approach Dr Oliveira and what to say to him.

A knock on a door.

OLIVEIRA (*inside*). Who is it?
  (*Paul enters the room.*)
  You know that the sick are not admitted here.
PAUL. I'm not sick, Dr Oliveira, and even if I were I should come in.
OLIVEIRA (*coldly*). I don't understand.
PAUL. Well, listen to me, then.
OLIVEIRA. What's the meaning of that suitcase?
PAUL. I've been here three years now.
OLIVEIRA. Not quite three years.
PAUL. The red patches I had at first disappeared after a few months.
OLIVEIRA. That doesn't mean anything.
PAUL. Since that time I've found nothing on me that would indicate leprosy.
OLIVEIRA. You've been here two years and seven months.
PAUL. And you've never once taken the trouble to examine me.
OLIVEIRA. You were examined by an expert.
PAUL. An expert in snakebites.
OLIVEIRA. With our equipment here we could never have arrived at such an exact diagnosis. You know that whoever has leprosy once will never be rid of it. Appearances are deceptive. There are cases that take a very long time to become acute.

PAUL. That may be, Dr Oliveira. But it isn't a medical discussion I want to have with you.

OLIVEIRA. What other kind of discussion, then?

PAUL. About experts and specialists. About Dr Bayard, who has spent the last three years –

OLIVEIRA (*quickly*). Not when you were examined.

PAUL. Nor when he prescribed hot baths for snake-bite. It's on the strength of a madman's report that I've been kept here for three years.

OLIVEIRA. I've already told you –

PAUL. Two years and seven months, and what I propose is that we leave it at that.

OLIVEIRA. Leave it at that?

PAUL. You'll make out a certificate for me, dated from today.

OLIVEIRA. That's blackmail.

PAUL. You may call it what you like. But do what I tell you – in your own interest.

OLIVEIRA. And is it in your interest too?

PAUL. I shouldn't make any claims.

OLIVEIRA. What do you want to get out for?

PAUL. I shall take the next boat.

OLIVEIRA. The next boat, of course. One always thinks that travelling will get one further.

PAUL. Everything has only begun.

OLIVEIRA. Be glad, then, that it's only just begun. Everything is much worse when it's drawing to an end.

PAUL. When it's drawing to an end. But it's going on. I'm well.

OLIVEIRA. Look around you in the world: how difficult it is for someone who hasn't got leprosy.

PAUL (*laughs*). It's easy for you to talk.

OLIVEIRA. Everything becomes easy for the man who has found certainty.

PAUL. It was the wrong word that brought me here.

OLIVEIRA. This is the place you were able to reach.

PAUL. The wrong word, to the wrong place. I must look for the right one.

OLIVEIRA. You fool. Go ahead and travel, then, if you think you'll find it elsewhere. Here's your certificate.

PAUL. Goodbye, Dr Oliveira.

(*The door opens and shuts.*)

PAUL (*narrating*). Yes, that was the last word I would say to him. Goodbye, Dr Oliveira. It was all as simple as that. He wouldn't make many difficulties because he wouldn't dare. Then would come the wonderful moment when I walked out past the porter, and I would show him my certificate, and then there would be the palm grove and the view of the sea, and perhaps one might already see one of the ships –

I awoke from these daydreams into which I had fallen before my half-packed suitcase. I awoke with a sudden pain, it was like a knife-thrust that cut my dreams in half and slipped on into my heart.

It was the thought that none of the inmates must see me. I must creep out when I went to see Dr Oliveira, I must lay a finger on my lips when I passed the porter, and steal away in the cover of the shrubs.

But would that be the end of it? Even if I sailed off, in the boat, over the sea, to freedom – was not my only certainty the knowledge that I'd forsaken the others? Would I be sailing to freedom? Could there still be caresses without venom and words that gave me joy? I remembered that O'Connor was losing strength rapidly, and Juanita was pregnant, that in a few weeks' time we should be putting on our play, and that I'd promised Manuela to whitewash her cell for her. Professor Fervao was waiting for me to read him the seventh canto of the *Lusiads*, and something had to be done to amuse Jorge, whose wife had got a divorce. Feliz told me last night that Juanita's baby was his, and Maria wouldn't be capable of doing the washing-up much longer, as she had suddenly got worse. True, they could all die well enough without me, but I couldn't live without them.

'*Unreal*' acoustic.

OLIVEIRA. One always thinks that travelling will get one further. This is the place you were able to reach.

PAUL (*narrating*). Who had said that? No, not Dr Oliveira. Myself. Someone was calling me, a woman's voice, probably it was Manuela. I unpacked the case again. There wasn't much to unpack, a pair of shoes, three shirts, a pair of trousers, five handkerchiefs, four pairs of socks – not much, but it was enough. Then Manuela called me again. I went out to ask her what she wanted.

SELECTED BIBLIOGRAPHY

A list of the principal works of Günter Eich, with the date
of their first appearance

Poems

ABGELEGENE GEHÖFTE (Kurt Schauer, Frankfurt,
1948)

BOTSCHAFTEN DES REGENS (Suhrkamp, Frankfurt, 1955)

ZU DEN AKTEN (Suhrkamp, Frankfurt, 1964)

ANLÄSSE UND STEINGÄRTEN (Suhrkamp, Frankfurt, 1966)

AUSGEWÄHLTE GEDICHTE (Suhrkamp, 1960)

Radio plays

TRÄUME (Suhrkamp, 1953)

STIMMEN (Suhrkamp, 1958)

IN ANDEREN SPRACHEN (Suhrkamp, 1964)

UNTER WASSER/BÖHMISCHE SCHNEIDER (Suhrkamp, 1964)

THE AUTHOR

Günter Eich was born in 1907 at Lebus on the Oder and studied Law and Oriental Languages at the universities of Leipzig, Paris and Berlin. He was a pioneer of the radio play in Germany, writing his first one in 1929. At the same time he became known as a poet, though his best work did not appear until after the war. From 1932 until his conscription he lived as a writer in Berlin. Then he served in the Army and was taken prisoner by the Americans. A number of his best-known poems of that period were written in the prisoner-of-war camp. After his release in 1946 he became prominent as a poet and radio dramatist. Since the war he has lived mainly in Bavaria, but has also travelled widely in Europe, Africa and America. In 1953 he married the Austrian novelist and poet Ilse Aichinger. Eich has been awarded many distinguished prizes, both for his poems and for his radio plays. Five of his radio plays have been broadcast in English translations, and his other work is represented in several anthologies published in Britain and America.